The Lands of the Bible

A RESOURCE FOR STUDYING SCRIPTURE
AND A COMPANION FOR TRAVELING IN

The Lands of the Bible:

- Israel
- The Palestinian Territories
- Sinai and Egypt
- Jordan
- Notes on Syria and Lebanon
- Comments on the Arab-Israeli Wars and the Palestinian Refugees
- The Clash of Cultures

Gerald L. Borchert

2011 – REVISED

Mossy Creek Press   Cleveland, Tennessee

Gerald L. Borchert, PhD (Princeton Theological Seminary), LLB (University of Alberta Law School), was Seminary Dean and Professor of New Testament (twice retired) and is currently Senior Professor at Carson Newman College. Dr. Borchert is also Thesis Director for the Robert E. Webber Institute for Worship Studies.

Mossy Creek Press
121 Holly Trail Road, NW
Cleveland, Tennessee 37311

The Lands of the Bible: Israel, the Palestinian Territories, Sinai & Egypt, Jordan, Notes on Syria & Lebanon, Comments on the Arab-Israeli Wars & the Palestinian Refugees, The Clash of Cultures. Revised edition.
© 1974, 1994, 1998, 2011 by Gerald L. Borchert. All rights reserved.
Published 2011.
Printed in the United States of America.
ISBN 978-1-936912-00-1

To order additional copies of this book, contact:

Mossy Creek Press
1-423-475-7308
www.parsonsporchbooks.com

Mossy Creek Press is an imprint of Parson's Porch Books

CONTENTS

ILLUSTRATIONS

AN HISTORICAL AND GEOGRAPHICAL RESOURCE for the study of scripture and a companion for visiting the lands of the Bible is an indispensable tool for the Christian. But even more significant is a pilgrimage involving a seminar in which one is actually able to study and visit the Bible lands in person. As Christians we can be greatly enriched by becoming better acquainted with the actual places that are part of our spiritual heritage. These places can become for us significant witnesses to the events that changed forever the course of history. What happened in the lands of the Bible has become important in the history of humanity and it should be extremely significant to each one who has taken the name of Jesus the Christ.

As you consider these lands and—one hopes—travel in the places where Abraham journeyed, where Moses wandered, where David and Solomon ruled, and where above all else the Lord Jesus was born and lived, you should be reminded again and again that as Christians we are a family of pilgrims who are bound together by the love of God manifested in us through the person of Jesus and the presence of Holy Spirit. A travel experience in these lands can afford you with a deeper perception of the Holy Scriptures and bring you into a fuller understanding of the ministry of Jesus. In such a pilgrimage you should have the opportunity to explore places that have been seared into the history of the people of God. Expect to be inspired as you visit the settings where Jesus walked and ministered to people in the turning days of the world's calendar. I have often told my students that such an adventure will alter the way you read the Bible and can be a strategic addition to a seminary education or other religious studies.

As you reflect on the lands of the Bible or actually visit them, some of which Christians have designated as the "Holy Land," I rejoice that you have allowed me to join you in this time of reflection through the use of this little guide. I trust that you will come to realize that I love the Mediterranean world since I have been in that region about forty times (by now having lost actual count). I have taught in both Israel and Egypt, camped in the Sinai before there were hotels, ridden a donkey into Petra, led Educational Opportunities' first group to the Valley of the Kings in Egypt, and flown over many sites with a photographer so that some of these places seem to feel like they are a second home to me. I pray, even though these lands have been involved in disputes for many centuries and the fertile crescent has indeed been the subject of many battles for millennia, that your study and/or being part of a Bible Lands Seminar will become more than a journey through history and geography. For those of you who are able to visit these lands I trust the journey will become for you an unforgettable experience that transcends wars and rumors of wars.

This little study book has been written to provide you with a simple introduction to your study of the lands of the Bible. It could have been much longer, more detailed and covered scores of other sites. It could have contained more than the few pictures I necessarily selected from the hundreds I have in my files. But along with your Bibles and other materials that you will acquire, it should provide you with a good deal of introductory historical and scriptural information to assist you in better understanding the places about which you have heard and you can visit. Hopefully for those of you who are able to travel to the lands of the Bible, this little guide will also serve as a continuing resource to remind you of the sites that you saw first hand and for others provide a useful tool for your further study of the Bible.

Of course, this preface is also the place for acknowledging my gratitude to others who have been important in the development of my thinking and understanding of the biblical lands throughout the years. These persons include Dr. G. Douglas Young, the founding principal of the Institute for Holy Land Studies, now called the Jerusalem University College. He invited me to become the first Visiting Professor at the Institute while I was serving on the Board of Trustees of the school (other visitors before me were designated as chaplains, but I was allowed to teach there). My gratitude goes to Dr. Richard Cleave, who allowed me to accompany him as he flew at low levels over Israel and the Sinai taking pictures of the various sites. Moreover, I am indebted to my former colleague in doctoral studies at Princeton, Dr. Abd-el M. Istafanous, who invited me to teach in the Reformed Seminary in Cairo. I must also mention the many guides from whom I have learned a great deal and the multiple travel agents who have helped in my journeys and have patiently made the arrangements for the many groups that I have led to the lands of the Bible. Particularly, I would acknowledge Dr. Jim Ridgeway of Educational Opportunities and the late Dr. Wayne Dehoney and his efficient daughter Kathy, the President of the Bible Lands and the Dehoney Travel Agency, both of whom and their staffs have gone the extra miles to change itineraries in order to suit my purposes in showing Christian pilgrims the most cogent aspects of that part of the world. I must also add to this list of acknowledgments the government travel offices and others in the various countries of Israel, Egypt, Jordan, and Syria who have supplied me with maps for this little work. With their approval, I have clipped or enhanced slightly many of these maps for the convenience of my readers. To all of these persons and their organizations I stand in deep gratitude.

To my readers of this work and seminar companions who have traveled and will travel with me and others, I pray that your reading of the Bible may be more enhanced through this work and hope (if you have not done so as yet) that when you are able to experience journeying in the lands of the Bible, it might be more spiritually enriching than you have even anticipated. As a result, may you also give all praise and glory to the Lord God for what you might learn and continue to learn. Moreover, may you seek to embody more fully the spirit of Christ Jesus because of having studied in a focused manner, walked where Jesus walked, and experienced enlightening encounters in the lands of the Bible.

Finally, I dedicate this little work to my dear wife who has suffered patiently my many trips to this part of the world and thankfully has accompanied me on a number of them.

Gerald L. Borchert

I

THE LANDS OF THE BIBLE AND PILGRIMAGE

　　　　　　　　　　　　　　　　　　　　　　　　　　　　Gerald L. Borchert

T HE LANDS OF THE BIBLE and especially Israel exert a phenomenal tug on the lives of Christians. In the heart of most of us there is a longing to see the landscapes and locations where the events of the Bible actually took place. But our goal is not merely to be tourists; we need rather to be pilgrims like Egeria who in the early Byzantine period sought and found a Christian meetinghouse that she believed was the home of Peter's mother-in-law. Her diary indicates that her pilgrimage to these lands was life transforming.

ISRAEL AND ITS NEIGHBORS

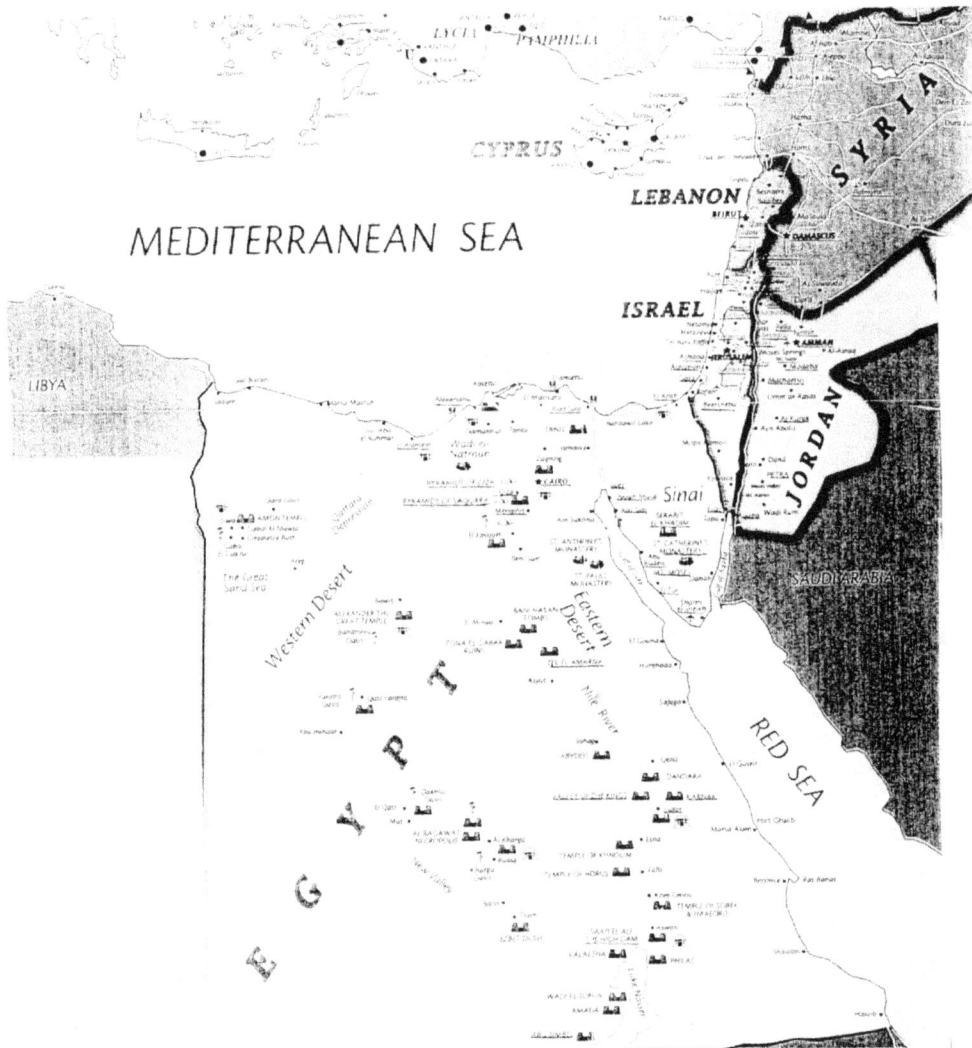

Tourists follow a set schedule to make sure that they see everything on the itinerary and they take pictures so that they can prove that they have been in those places. They hurry quickly through museums and visit historical sites before moving on to the next place. Pilgrims visit the Lands of the Bible not only to see the places like tourists where significant events have taken place but they also seek prayerfully to encounter God in those places. Tourists do not expect that their lives will change substantially because of their visits. Pilgrims anticipate that their lives will be affected because they have stood in what they consider to be "holy places."

Why is this region of the world such a magnet not only for pilgrims but also for tourists? Is it not because even tourists have a sense that God somehow became more apparent not only in the unfolding of the divine story through the Patriarchs and Matriarchs like Abraham and Sarah, the Judges like Deborah and Gideon, the Prophets like Jeremiah and Hosea but most concretely in the one and only Son of God, Jesus the Christ? As Christians in our studies of the Bible, we have become acquainted with people like Abraham, Moses, David, Elijah, Isaiah, John the Baptist, Jesus's mother Mary, Peter, and Paul. Of course, we have also stumbled over strange sounding names of places and people. We have also sometimes wondered what it would have been like to be present near Mt. Carmel when Elijah called down fire from heaven, or at Jerusalem when Solomon built the Temple, or in Nazareth when Jesus was a youth, or in Bethlehem when Jesus was born and the family had to flee, or at Caesarea Maritima when Paul stood before Herod Agrippa, or on the Sea of Galilee when Jesus called Peter to get out of the boat and walk on the water.

If you can visit Israel, your time will be encompassed with new insights as a result of standing in the various sites. Israel may seem to be a huge place in your mental conceptions but it is hardly the size of the state of Massachusetts. From Dan to Beer Sheba is scarcely 200 miles in length, and at its maximum width Israel is a mere sixty miles from the Mediterranean to the Jordan River. Yet the mountains and valleys make the distances seem far, far greater. This historic land stands between the two ancient superpowers of Egypt in the south and the Mesopotamian kingdoms in the north. The fact that this area is also known as the Fertile Crescent means that Israel stands in the center as the narrow land bridge between the Mediterranean Sea on the west and the dessert on the east.

Biblical history will come alive when you can stand at Megiddo, gaze at the Canaanite altar and realize that the Tel has witnessed more than twenty destructions so that the city became the symbol of the great judgment of God and the final destruction. Or, you will be surprised when you encounter the huge Tel at Beth Shan where the bodies of Saul and Jonathan were hung on the city wall as a sign of desecration by their enemies and then gasp at the contrast between the Tel and the incredible ruins of the Roman city in the valley that are still being uncovered by archaeologists today. Our knowledge concerning the Lands of the Bible continues to grow.

But beyond such knowledge, expect to grow in your personal understanding of your faith when you are able to walk down the *Via Dolorosa* (Way of Sorrows) in Jerusalem and ponder the suffering of our Lord at the hands of political manipulators and a hostile mob. Or, you will certainly be moved to reflect on the fact that some of those ancient olive trees in the Garden of Gethsemane probably were there and their older branches witnessed the agony of Jesus as he prayed for strength to endure his immanent crucifixion and later they survived the devastating destruction of Jerusalem in A.D. 70. Visiting the Lands of the Bible can be a paradoxical experience because as you come to visit places important in the past you can become transformed in the present.

When Nathaniel learned that Jesus had come from Nazareth, he asked Philip, "Can any good come out of [that unimportant town of] Nazareth?" Philip wisely replied, "Come and See" (John 1:43–46)! Today you are challenged to Come as a Pilgrim to the Lands of the Bible and see the places where God has acted to change many lives and the course of world history.

II

ARCHAEOLOGY

TABLE 2.1

A BASIC OUTLINE OF ARCHAEOLOGICAL PERIODS IN ISRAEL

Old Stone Age	Prior to 10,000 B.C.
Middle Stone Age	10,000 to 8000 B.C.
Late Stone Age (Neolithic)	8000 to 4500 (or 4000) B.C.
Copper/Bronze Age (Chalcolithic, or Æneolithic)	4500 to 3150 B.C.
Early Bronze Age	3200 to 2200 (2100) B.C.
Middle Bronze Age	2200 to 1550 B.C.
Late Bronze Age	1550 to 1200 B.C.
Early Iron Age	1200 to 950 B.C.
Middle Iron Age	950 to 586 B.C.
Late Iron Age (Babylonian/Persian Period)	586 to 333 B.C.
Hellenistic Period	333 to 63 B.C.
Roman Period	63 B.C. to A.D. 323
Byzantine Period	A.D. 323 to 636
Islamic Period	A.D. 636 to 1917

The Contemporary Periods

The Period of the Mandate	A.D. 1917 to 1948
The Divided Levant	A.D. 1948 to the present

ARCHAEOLOGY AND THE BIBLE

THE WORK OF ARCHAEOLOGISTS has fascinated students of the Bible for many years. This fascination is in large measure due to the fact that it has allowed us to increase our understanding of the biblical texts and the biblical world. Even though some people have viewed archaeology as a means of proving aspects of "truth" related to their faith, the role of archaeology is primarily aimed at enlightening our understanding of life in the ancient world, contexts for peoples' movements, and structures that they built. These structures and the objects that are uncovered—such as broken pottery, coins, and inscriptions—provide the kinds of information that enable us to posit conclusions concerning a people's social patterns. In some rare cases, documents or clay tablets are discovered that offer written insights into their thoughts and activities. The opening of tombs, even if they have been disturbed by grave robbers—such as those of the Egyptian Pharaohs and their supporters or of Philip of Macedon—supply items related to peoples' actual lives and expectations concerning their views of a future life.

Biblical archaeology has passed through dramatic changes in the last few decades. The use of computers and modern scientific methods has greatly enhanced the work of archaeologists. Today, a wide range of experts are involved in the study of artifacts and materials. In addition, even before any digging is begun, modern surveying methods are employed including topographical and aerial surveying. (Believe me, I learned a great deal in flying over Israelite sights in a small plane at a low level.) Then, designated small sections of a **Tel** (an artificial mound which has been built up as the result of multiple layers of habitation and destruction) are marked out for excavation. Naturally, the deeper archaeologists cut down through the levels of a Tel, the earlier will be the occupational period being examined. Megiddo is an example of a Tel that experienced more than twenty different levels of life.

Today, when archaeologists excavate a site, field supervisors meticulously record all the details related to the digging of shafts into the Tel, and any findings that are discovered are measured and photographed. Precise records are kept of any artifacts that are discovered. Even minute artifacts are logged, because once a section of a site is excavated, there is no further excavation possible. When Dame Kenyon officially excavated Jericho, archaeology was in its infant stage, and such procedures were not always followed. Indeed, dirt that was removed from one place on the Tel was dumped elsewhere on the Tel so that it is now not productive to do any further work on the site. Moreover, mud bricks do not last long in the weather, so visitors to the site are usually disappointed in not being able to see the fallen walls of Jericho. But archaeologists today are much more attuned to their task and even use medical scanning devices to read clay tablets without destroying the clay covers that were made to protect them. All these records then provide the basis for further archaeological campaigns.

In the past, archaeologists were primarily interested in the collection of monuments and artifacts. Today, archaeologists are concerned with establishing greater clarity on the patterns of daily life and the customs of the ancients. For example, the carbonized remains of seeds found in storage jars or on threshing floors can be examined by botanists, microbiologists, and paleobotanists to assist in the determination of the dietary patterns of the ancient inhabitants of a region. Medical specialists are employed in evaluating skeletal remains and funerary procedures to provide insights into physical and social patterns of the early Semites. These specialized studies assist us in visualizing a more authentic picture of the people of the Bible and their customs. They enable us to understand them better as genuine human beings who actually lived in history, worked hard to eke out a living, exemplified faith and also made great mistakes, suffered from wars, famine and disease, and followed certain prescribed social customs—just as we do. As a result, they become more readily recognizable as real people, not as paper dolls in an ancient story and not merely as constructs of theological suppositions.

But much of the work of archaeologists also suffers from severe limitations. Information is often very fragmentary and incomplete. Physical remains are scattered and many of the important artifacts make their way to the antiquities markets for sale and their exact provenance or original context is in fact lost. Such is the case concerning the authenticity of the "James Ossuary"* that has recently raised such a debate among some scholars. For this reason, Christians should not expect archaeology to "prove" the existence any particular biblical person or event mentioned in the Bible. Believers do not need archaeology to understand that God loves the world or that the Bible is the Word of God. Approximately a century earlier, archaeologist John Garstang sought to prove the truth of the Bible by excavating Jericho and seeking the actual wall; however, later archaeologists examined pottery, building styles, and the levels of occupation at the Tel and concluded that Garstang's speculations were clearly erroneous.

In visiting sites such as Megiddo, Beth Shan, Caesarea Maritima, Jerusalem, and elsewhere, believers today may not gain all the information they would like to possess in order to prove convincingly events connected with the conquest of Ai or the travels of Abraham but they do not need such information to know that the God of Abraham actually exists. They are certainly able to ride in a boat on the Sea of Galilee, but they cannot duplicate Jesus walking on that deep lake in the midst of a storm. Control over such winds and water is not an aspect of human power. Such power is a quality of the divine and was vested particularly in God's only Son. Walking on dry land where Jesus walked, however, can be a very significant life-altering experience that does not require an archaeological degree. But the sites that have been uncovered by archaeologists can indeed be visited today and they can remind us of strategic events in the past that are able to enrich our lives in the present. Such is the goal of those who today would follow the early pilgrims in their trek through the lands of the Bible.

While many discoveries have been made in or through the work of archaeology during the last century, each discovery must be carefully interpreted not by the popular new media but by the careful weighing of all the evidence connected with the discovery. Welcome then to the lands where archaeology has been in the forefront of human interest and research.

* The "James Ossuary" is thought to be the limestone box in which are stored the bones of James, the brother of Jesus.

III

ABOUT TRADITION AND LANGUAGE

TRADITION AND TRADITIONAL

T HE VISITOR TO THE Lands of the Bible should become conversant with certain terms that are used by archaeologists, historians and guides. Among the most important of these terms is the word "tradition" or "traditional." It is a term that is to be distinguished from words like "fact" or "historically proven reality." Traditional as used in connection with a site as we shall see represents an ancient belief, perception or reminiscence that is intended to identify a particular site with a particular event in the past (such as the sites for the Sermon of the Mount or the multiplication of loaves and fish). These traditional sites point to events but even though scholars seek to verify the connection between the sites and the events, certainty is not possible. Sometimes a site was chosen for the sake of convenience when those who chose it did not know the actual site.

No one, for example, would question that the Sea of Galilee (Tiberias, Chinneroth, Kinneret) to be an indisputable reality. But the site of the feeding of the five thousand at Tabgha is a traditional site that dates back to the time of Queen Helena (the mother of Constantine) who built chapels and churches at sites that she sought to identify at the time. Other sites around the Sea of Galilee are likewise traditional sites even though they may be beautifully adorned like the traditional site of the Sermon on the Mount, which has a picturesque octagonal chapel designed by the famous Italian architect Antonio Barluzzi. The site of Kursi, where the healing of the demoniac and the destruction of the bewitched herd of pigs occurred, is likewise traditional.* In contrast, the cities of Capernaum and Chorazin/Korazin are hardly in dispute and the third-fourth century synagogue of Capernaum almost certainly was built over the site of the earlier synagogue where Jesus

---

* * For a helpful example of how scholars weigh the legitimacy of this traditional site see the discussion on Gadara in the section on Jordan.

must have worshiped and dialoged with the people. The nearby site designated as the home of Peter's mother-in-law should be viewed as traditional, although the site was clearly a fifth century worship center which was built over a much earlier home which early Christians may have constructed to remember a healing by Jesus which took place there.

When one journeys south to Jerusalem, there are a number of sites which represent similar distinctions. There is no doubt that the Temple Mount is fixed because the Herodian stones make such a location clear and those familiar with the area can identify some of the stones that likely go back to the time of Solomon. There is a question, however, concerning whether or not the stone at the center of the Dome of the Rock actually goes back to the place where Abraham attempted to sacrifice Isaac (a Jewish tradition) or Ishmael (a Muslim tradition).

The sites of the crucifixion and burial of Jesus offer another example. The Garden Tomb is a place which Protestants love to visit in spite of the fact that it is a very recent tradition dating back only to the time of the British General Gordon. When he was sitting on the wall of Jerusalem, he viewed a nearby cliff and thought it looked like a skull. Nearby he found an ancient tomb and a tradition was born. The tradition connected with the Church of the Holy Sepulchre has a much longer history dating back to the time of Queen Helena. The Church of the Nativity in Bethlehem is also dependent upon the selection of Queen Helena. These traditions of Helena are in turn dependent upon evidence available to her in the fourth century following the destruction of Jerusalem and its rebuilding as the Roman city of *Aelia Capitolina*.

In contrast, the sites of Jericho, Masada and the Dead Sea are hardly in question. The site of Qumran is not in question, although there is considerable debate about what was its original purpose. Was it a monastery containing a scriptorium, or was it a building designed for industry? Is the building connected to the fact that the nearby cliffs contained ancient biblical scrolls? Scholars have debated these questions. But a more interesting point involves the site of the Caravansary of the Good Samaritan on the old road between Jerusalem and Jericho. The name is certainly a construct developed from the parable by Jesus and has nothing to do directly with the life of Jesus. Of course, there may have been stopping places that served for refreshment and protection in the hostile valley between the two cities, but the parable (the story) undoubtedly gave the name to the place and thus became a tradition.

In designating a site to be traditional, scholars are not normally declaring that such a site should be regarded as false or constructed (except in the previous case) but they are indicating that a direct connection between an event and a site is not sustainable. Visitors to those sites, however, should regard them as memorials of important biblical events. In addition, one should remember that those sites protected the areas from being used for other purposes.

LANGUAGE: SEMITIC VOWELS AND WORDS

Readers who are unfamiliar with the nature of Semitic languages like Hebrew and Arabic should understand that vowels may not remain constant in names and may change with use so that one may find different spelling of the names of people and places. Moreover, some of the consonants have been difficult for people to pronounce and as a result related sounds are substituted. For example, the "P" in the name for the Greek god "Pan" was difficult for the Arabic-speaking people of northern Palestine to pronounce, so after the Roman period inhabitants returned to using the earlier Greek name Panaeus (or Panias) for Caesarea Philippi. "Panaeus" became "Banias" instead because of difficulties in pronunciation.

I have therefore tried to be sensitive to those who might become confused by the various place names that are used throughout this book. Accordingly, in order to assist the reader, I frequently give alternative spellings for names—or indeed alternative names—where there might be both Greek and Semitic names used for a place or person.

IV

A HISTORICAL SKETCH CONCERNING THE LAND OF ISRAEL

THE LAND OF ISRAEL: SELECTED HISTORIC PARK SITES
(The numbers below are coordinated with those on the National Parks Maps)

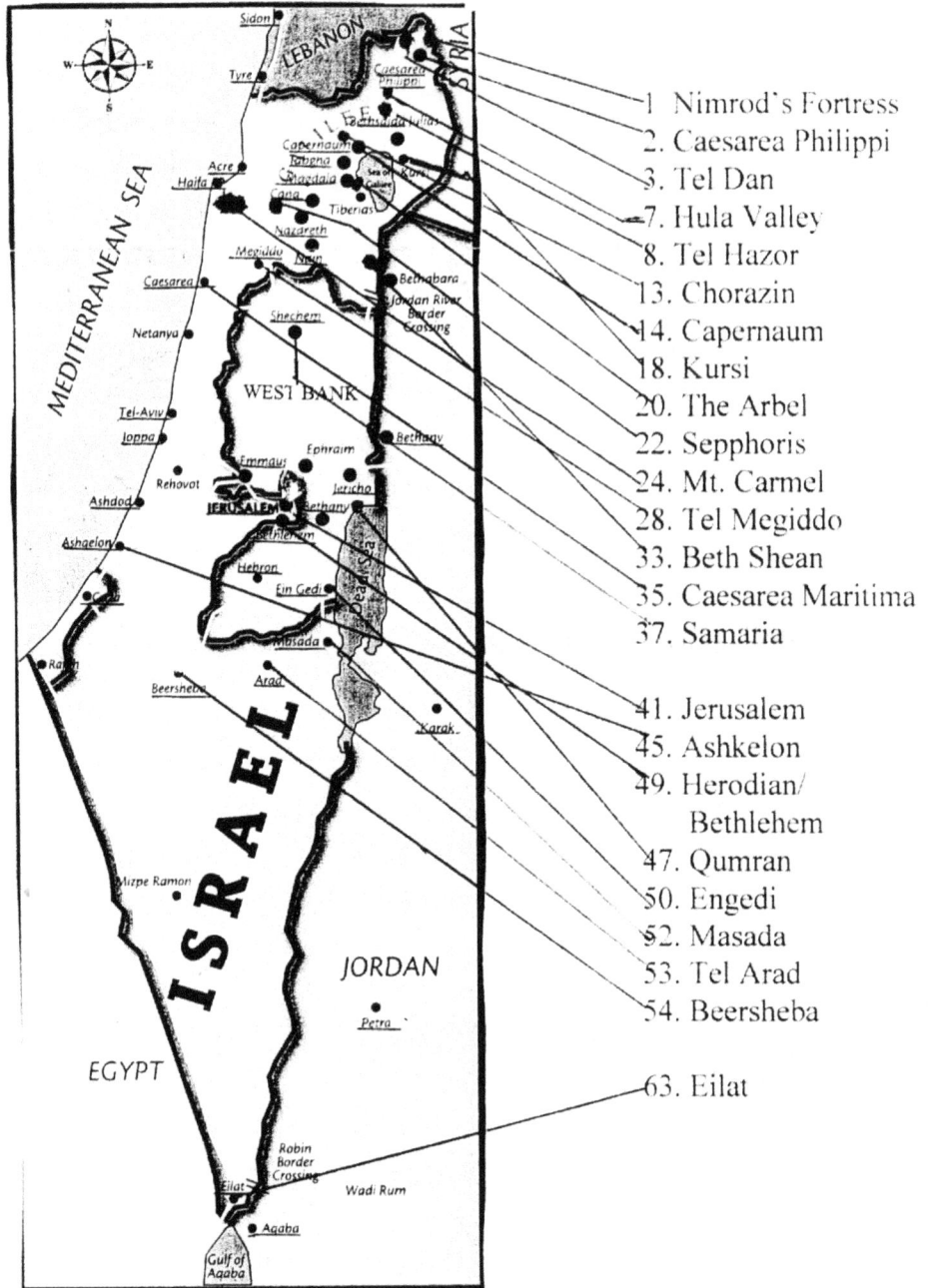

1 Nimrod's Fortress
2. Caesarea Philippi
3. Tel Dan
7. Hula Valley
8. Tel Hazor
13. Chorazin
14. Capernaum
18. Kursi
20. The Arbel
22. Sepphoris
24. Mt. Carmel
28. Tel Megiddo
33. Beth Shean
35. Caesarea Maritima
37. Samaria

41. Jerusalem
45. Ashkelon
49. Herodian/ Bethlehem
47. Qumran
50. Engedi
52. Masada
53. Tel Arad
54. Beersheba

63. Eilat

NAMING THE LAND[1]

G EOGRAPHICALLY, THE NAME ASSOCIATED with the area from Dan to Beer Sheba, which became the home of Israel after the Exodus, was known as **Canaan** ("**land of purple**"—see also Lebanon for Phoenicia). In the Old Testament it designated the land of the Canaanites, a general term for the original inhabitants of the area. According to Genesis 9:18 and 10:15–18, Canaan was the son of Ham, one of the three sons of Noah and the father of: the Sidonians, the Hittites, the Jebusites, the Amorites, the Girgashites, the Hivites, etc. These names appear later as nations that occupied the land prior to the conquest in the days of Joshua (Exod 3:17, Deut 7:1, and Josh 3:10).

The region of the Fertile Crescent where Israel lived is technically known as **the Levant** and has for centuries been termed "**Palestine**." This latter name is derived from the name "Philistines" (the Hebrew *pelisthim*) and the Greek historian Herodotus apparently first applied the name to Canaan. The **Philistines** were a "People of the Sea" (**Phoenicians** from the Greek *phoinos* "reddish-purple"), but their origin is still debated. These Philistines sought to invade Egypt in the eighth year of Ramses III (ca. 1188 B.C.) but they were unsuccessful and in a concluding covenant with Egypt were allowed to settle along the Mediterranean coast in the lower Levant, the area thereafter being designated as "the land of the Philistines" or "Philistia" (cf. Gen 21:32, 34; Exod 13:17 and 15:14). The five major cities of the Philistines (Pentapolis) were Gaza, Ashkelon, Ashdod, Ekron and Gath (cf. Josh 12:3). The Romans, particularly Hadrian, designated the area of Judea as a Roman sub-province of Syria called *Provincia Palestina*. That term became the official name for the entire area of Israel by the fourth century A.D.

THE LAND AND A BRIEF HISTORY

From the Exodus to the Romans

Following the departure (Exodus) from Egypt and after the death of Moses, the Israelites under Joshua conquered large sections of this land (Canaan west of the Jordan) as well as sections east of the Jordan (Josh 1:12–15) and they divided the territory among the twelve tribes (Num 34:16–29; Josh 13:1–19:51). The tribe of Levi settled among the

---

1. For further information on the history and the land of Israel, see Gerald L. Borchert, *Jesus of Nazareth: Background, Witnesses, and Significance* (Macon: Mercer University Press, forthcoming).

other tribes as a reminder of God's presence and importance among all the people (Num 35:1–8; Josh 21:1–42), and the Joseph tribe was divided and given two allotments because of Jacob's adoption of the two sons of Joseph and Joseph's position among his brothers (Gen 48:5–6 and 49:22–26; Josh 16:1–18). But the Israelites were unable to conquer all the territories and they lived among the former inhabitants of the land, often **adopting their worship practices**. The tribe of **Dan** was not able to conquer its territory among the Philistines and so the tribe moved north and wiped out the inhabitants of Laish, renaming the area Dan (Judg 18:27–29). In the time of Samuel the land of Canaan was already known as the "land of Israel" (1 Sam 13:9).

The united kingdom that David forged was shattered after the death of Solomon in **922** B.C. Then Jeroboam, the first ruler of the Northern Kingdom, sought to isolate Israel from the Southern kingdom of Judah (which included the tribe of Simeon) and the influence of the Temple in Jerusalem by establishing independent worship centers at Bethel and at Dan (1 Kgs 12:28–29). The prophets forcefully condemned these worship centers and Jeroboam was regarded as a symbol of a renegade, heretical ruler. Archaeologists have recently uncovered the worship center at Dan, and visiting it provides a stark reminder of the temptation to **syncretism** (the joining of several commitments together in worship and life).

The Northern Kingdom with its capital at Samaria was much more unstable than the South and witnessed **changes in dynastic leadership** frequently. The prophets continually condemned the false worship practices and predicted the coming of the judgment of God. The Northern Kingdom (Israel) thus suffered continual harassment from its powerful neighbors and it became a vassal state to Assyria. Finally, after a series of episodes, Samaria fell to Sargon II in **722** B.C. and many of the people were forcefully carried to other provinces under Assyrian control. In their place the **Assyrians** imported other people, and the Israelites that remained in the land soon intermarried with the others and ceased to exist as an independent people.

The Southern Kingdom lasted considerably longer, and under a smattering of more faithful kings from the dynasty of David, like Hezekiah and Josiah, the people were able to sustain their independence for more than another century. But Babylon, which was the new power in Mesopotamia, finally conquered Judah, and Jerusalem fell in **587–586** B.C. to the forces of Nebuchadnezzar (2 Chr 36:17–19). The pattern of the conquering **Babylonians** was quite different than that of the Assyrians. The Babylonians carried most of the artisans and educated people to Babylon, but they allowed them to settle in separate areas so the Jews were able to continue as an independent group while serving the Babylonian captors. As a result, the Jews flourished in Babylonia and developed a highly structured and effective social system, so much so that when Cyrus and the Persians conquered the Babylonians and permitted the Jews to return to the Levant, many Jews chose to stay in Mesopotamia.

Those who returned to Jerusalem and the Levant rebuilding the Temple and the Walls under **Ezra and Nehemiah** then began to reestablish Jewish communities throughout the region in the post-exilic period. Not only were the priesthood and the Levitical clans reconfigured but also their roles were reestablished in relation to the Temple. A new and powerful institution of the Synagogue with highly trained rabbinic scholars as the official interpreters of the Jewish scriptures also emerged during the Exile and took firm roots in Israelite society.

The world then saw the rise of a powerful superpower in Macedonia as **Alexander the Great** came on the scene, and in **331 B.C.** he conquered Palestine and took over the entire region from Antioch in Syria to Egypt. But he died in Babylon and left no dynasty, so his generals divided his conquered territories. The **Ptolemies** in Egypt and the **Seleucids** in Mesopotamia constantly fought for control of the land bridge of Palestine. Finally, under the **Maccabees** and their **Hasmonean** successors, the Jews were able to withstand the pressures of the post-Alexandrine leadership in Egypt and Mesopotamia. The glory of Israel seemed to be returning. But the dream of a reborn Israel with the Hasmoneans was soon dashed.

The Roman Period

In **63 B.C.** another factor was inserted into the mix as Pompey and the Romans arrived in Jerusalem. The Romans (the *Kittim* of Dan. 11:30) usually watched for opportunities to join in situations where there were struggles and such was the case in Israel between Hyrcannus and Aristobulus, descendants of the once powerful Hasmoneans. The Romans sided with Hyrcannus but gave the actual administrative power to Antipater (a savvy Idumean strongman politician who was the father of Herod the Great).

Herod the Great, probably the most impressive **builder** of his time, spent his time organizing building projects throughout the province. Providing safe havens for himself was one of his goals, and among those fortresses were: (1) the **Tower of Antonio** in Jerusalem near the Temple (where some suggest Jesus was beaten and where Paul was undoubtedly held); (2) the **Triple Towers** also in Jerusalem near the current Jaffa Gate dedicated to Phasel (his brother), Hippicus (his close friend), and Mariamne (his favorite wife among the ten, whom he later murdered because of a suspected plot to unseat him); (3) the **Herodion**, near Bethlehem (where Herod was buried); (4) **Masada**, near the Dead Sea (which he used to protect Mariamne when he had to flee from the Jews and was later used by the Zealots); and (5) **Machaerus**, across the Jordan and in the desert (where John the Baptist was imprisoned), that provided an escape route from his enemies. Among his other projects were: (1) the magnificent seaport city of **Caesarea Maritima** (where Paul was imprisoned) with its incredible harbor and beautiful palace; (2) his winter palatial retreat near **Jericho**; and (3) a completely rebuilt Samaria which he called **Sebaste** in honor of Augustus, his patron.

But the rest of the story was downhill for the Jews until the **Fall of Jerusalem in A.D. 70**. Resistance of the Jews to Roman and Herodian rule continued to grow, and the Zealots (freedom fighters) began to emerge in both the north and the south. War broke out first around Caesarea Maritima and spread like wildfire in the north. **Vespasian**, the Roman commander, was dispatched by Nero from Antioch (the capital of the entire province of Syria) to quell the uprising with a huge force of 60,000 men, and he succeeded until Nero died. As the most powerful commander of his generation, Vespasian left Palestine immediately with his forces for Rome in order to claim the "Purple Robe." The Jews thought God had delivered them, but their hopes were short-lived because Vespasian sent his son **Titus** with an even lager force to completely subdue the Jews. The beautiful Temple of Herod suffered burning and destruction in the Fall of Jerusalem. Planning and building of the Temple had begun in **20/19 B.C.** and it was not finished until about **A.D. 63** (see the time notation of **forty-six years** in John 2:20 for a sense of the stage of building at that time). The Temple thus stood finished only for a very few years, perhaps as a symbol of judgment (cf. Mark 13:1–2). A triumphal march was given to Titus in Rome and a **triumphal arch** was erected in the Roman Forum in honor of that conquest. Then the Romans turned their attention to the Jewish resisters in the **Herodion** and **Masada** (the latter finally fell in A.D. 72) and those stories of courage have been used to inspire contemporary new **Jewish recruits** in their inductions into the Israeli military forces.

One might think that the story of resistance ended at that point but it did not! The Jews without a Temple turned their full attention to the interpretation of the Law and to the **condemning of Christians as heretics** in the Beth Din Councils of Yavneh during the next decades (see the Curse of the *Minim* that was added to the *Twelfth Benediction*[2]). The Jews were permitted some rebuilding but when Emperor **Hadrian** issued an edict in A.D. 132 forbidding circumcision, the Jews remembered the terrible years of persecution under Antiochus Ephiphanes and the Seleucids and saw visions of a new Maccabean uprising. A candidate came forth by the name of Simon, whom the prominent Rabbi Aqiba designated as **Bar Kokhba** (son of a star; cf. Num 24:17). He summoned the Jews to arms, and the ensuing battles were bloody; however, the Romans were the victors in A.D. 135. As a result, the Romans tore down any remaining vestiges of Judaism in Jerusalem, forbade the Jews from entering it, and rebuilt the city as a Roman Colony named *Aelia Capitolina* with Roman streets and temples. The Jews thus **lost control of Jerusalem** from that time until **1967**.

The Byzantine Period

The name "Palestine" does not actually convey the diversity of the inhabitants of the land where biblical Israel lived. The Fathers of the Church, however, accepted this Roman designation of Palestine for the land, and following **Constantine's Edict of Milan** in 313 A.D., which established toleration for Christianity, the Church blossomed and the doors were opened for changes in the Levant. **Queen Helena**, a fervent Christian and the mother of Constantine, then began her trek to the "Holy Land" and to the **identification of sites** that she determined should be revered. During this time (which is generally known as the beginning of the Byzantine Christian period) the construction of special churches and chapels began in order to mark the sites which Helena, to the best of her ability, identified in the fourth century and, with the resources of the empire at her disposal, believed could be associated with the ministry of Jesus. Even though many of these sites were later destroyed by Muslim conquerors, a number of their locations are today fairly certain. Most of them, however, are to be regarded in the best sense of the word as "traditional" because their direct connection with Jesus cannot always be proven. Nevertheless, for the early pilgrims their significance was that they were both accessible at the

---

2. For the curse of the "Nazarenes and the *minim*," see for example C. K. Barrett, *The New Testament Background: Selected Documents* (New York: Harper & Row, 1961), 166–67.

time and were important concrete reminders of the activities of Jesus.

Constantine died in 337, and his sons (Constans and Constantius) **split the empire in 340.** In 380 Theodosius, the eastern emperor, declared Christianity to be the official **state religion** in the east, and during the closing decades of the century **Jerome** was busy in Bethlehem translating the Bible afresh from Hebrew and Greek into Latin (The Vulgate). Indeed, undercover he learned Hebrew from a Jew during this time. Then during the **fifth century** the Western Empire was constantly under siege from hostile peoples (such as the Visigoths, Franks, and Vandals) who were moving westward into Europe and even managed to devastate Rome. **Justinian,** who came to power in the sixth century, tried to recoup some of the losses in the West and ordered that major improvements be made at some of the most important sites in Palestine. Particularly still evident is the fact that he enlarged the **Church of the Nativity in Bethlehem.**

The Persians, the Muslims, and the Crusaders

But the tide was turning, and the people south and east of the Mediterranean began to flex their muscles. The **Persians** moved west and north in A.D. 614 and sacked Damascus and Jerusalem, destroying or seriously damaging most of the standing Christian churches in Palestine and looting them of their sacred treasures. However, they made an **exception** with the Church of the Nativity in Bethlehem because of the beautiful mosaic on the entrance wall that portrayed the wise men that visited the baby Jesus. Then in 570, Muhammad was born, and after his death Abu Bakr united the tribes in Arabia (632–33) and his forces overran the land of Palestine, forcing the **collapse of Byzantine Christian power in Jerusalem by 640.**

As Islam continued to expand in the region, power shifted to Damascus, and the **Umayyad Caliphate** assumed control of the Levant from 661 to 750. It was during this period that Abd el Malik ordered the construction of the golden **Dome of the Rock** on the Temple Mount (685–705) in Jerusalem to commemorate what is believed by Muslims to be the site of Abraham's sacrifice of **Ishmael** (not Isaac) and the night ascent of Muhammad. Then power shifted several times more as the **Abbasids** from Baghdad gained control (750–936), followed by the **Ikhsidids** (to 969) and then the **Fatimids** who were in control when the Crusaders came on the Palestinian scene in 1096–99.

The period of the **Crusaders** was marked by calls in Europe for the freeing of "the Promised Land" from the hands of the so-called "infidel Muslims" and Jerusalem was finally conquered in **1099.** The Kurdish warrior, **Saladin,** soon emerged, however, as the leader of the Muslims (1169–1193) and replaced the Fatimids, founding in 1174 a new dynasty known as the **Ayyubids.** He summoned the Muslims to a Holy War (*jihād*) and in **1187** slaughtered the heavily armed Crusaders in the blistering Palestinian sun at the **Horns of Hattin** (an extinct volcanic plateau) as they were en route from Caesarea Maritima to resupply Jerusalem. The result was that even in the later Crusades the Europeans could not again reestablish Jerusalem as their capital.

The ferocious **Turkish Mamelukes** then assumed power in the Middle East in 1250 and held Jerusalem until the **Ottoman Turks** gained control in 1517. Since Jerusalem was the third most significant city for the Muslims after Mecca and Medina, **Suleiman the Magnificent** (1520–1566) ordered the rebuilding of the **walls of Jerusalem** that encompass today's "Old City." Some of these walls follow a different course than the older walls of the city and visitors to Jerusalem can distinguish the smaller stones of Suleiman's construction from those of the larger decorated Herodian stones.

The Mandate and the Current Situation

The Ottomans held control of the region until World War I when in **1917 the Allies** took control of the region and divided the **entire area into four sections (Syria, Transjordan, Palestine and Lebanon) and gave the British a Mandate over the territory of Palestine and the city of Jerusalem.** The French were allotted some areas in the northern Levant. Then, following the Second World War, the land was divided between the Palestinian inhabitants and the Israeli settlers, fulfilling the **promise the Allies made to the Jews** that they would be given a homeland called "Israel" for their support of the Allied cause and as a haven after the **holocaust of the Nazi genocide.**

The **Muslim world rejected the division in 1948, which was penned on a map of Palestine with a series of "Green Lines,"** and they vowed to push the Jews into the Mediterranean Sea when the British withdrew. The Muslims also vowed that **any Palestinian** who remained in the area when they went to war with Israel would be summarily dispatched. Thus, many Palestinians left their homes and crossed the borders particularly into Jordan and Lebanon and lived as **refugees** for many years awaiting their return to Palestine but not being given an actual homeland in the surrounding countries that had demanded that they leave their homes. But the Jews sustained their positions against the Muslim world in 1948 and the refugees were not granted rights of resettlement in Israeli territory because they had *abandoned their rights* to the land.

In **1967**, the Muslim world attacked Israel in what has become known as the "**Six Day War.**" Actually, it was not a *six*-day war but three "*two*-day" wars. Israel fought Egypt, Syria, and Jordan separately and was victorious on all three fronts, taking the Golan Heights from Syria and the Sinai from Egypt. Israel has since signed nonaggression pacts with Jordan and Egypt and returned the **Sinai** to Egypt, but it has not reached such an agreement with Syria. Moreover, because Syria used those mountains to fire rockets on the settlers around the Sea of Galilee, Israel has **refused to return the Golan cliffs** to Syria for the purposes of strategic protection.

What the future will hold is uncertain, but Israel is neither likely to give up Jerusalem as its capital nor allow it to be divided. The Palestinians earnestly desire to have full authority over their homeland and want Jerusalem as their capital. As long as terrorism continues, **the wall** that is under construction around the Palestinian territories will continue to be built, further isolating the Palestinians. The situation requires great sensitivity and wisdom beyond mere human politics. But Christians need to be aware that the **Christian inhabitants** in this segment of the Biblical Lands are particularly caught in a **squeeze** between the Israelis and the Palestinians. **Many are leaving** (emigrating from) their homeland because of unbelievable pressures and these Christians should be in our prayers. **Let us pray for the peace of Jerusalem and all Israel/Palestine** (cf. Ps 122:6). Such a prayer should be on the hearts of all Christians.[3]

TABLE 4.1

THE ROMAN EMPERORS[4]

Julius (Caesar) undisputed master	45–44 B.C.[5]

3. See also the further discussion on the Arab-Israeli Wars and the Refugee Problem.

4. For a comparison of the eight kings of Revelation to the Roman emperors—Augustus to Domitian—see Gerald Borchert, "Revelation" in *NLT Study Bible* (Carol Stream: Tyndale House, 2008), 2191.

5. In academic studies, B.C. = B.C.E. (Before the Common Era) and A.D. = C.E. (Common Era).

The Second Triumverate: Octavian, Mark Antony, and Aemilius Lepidus	ca. 44–27 B.C.
Augustus (Octavian)	27 B.C.–A.D. 14
Tiberius	A.D. 14–37
Gaius Caligula	A.D. 37–41
Claudius	A.D. 41–54
Nero	A.D. 54–68
Anarchy	A.D. 68–69
Vespasian	A.D. 69–79
Titus	A.D. 79–81
Domitian	A.D. 81–96
Nerva	A.D. 96–98
Trajan	A.D. 98–117
Hadrian	A.D. 117–138

TABLE 4.2

THE HERODIANS AND THE LAND OF ISRAEL

Antipater (the Father of Herod the Great)	
Herod the Great (King)	The Entire kingdom (40) 37–4 B.C.

(Herod the Great specified Archaelaus as his successor; however, the Romans did not trust him, divided the kingdom, and reduced the status of his sons.)

Herod Archaelaus (Ethnarch)	Judea and Samaria 4/3 B.C.–A.D. 6
Herod Antipas (Tetrarch)	Galilee and Perea 4/3 B.C.–A.D. 39
Herod Philip (Tetrarch)	Iturea and Trachonitis 4/3 B.C.–A.D. 34

[Roman Procurators controlled Judea and Samaria A.D. 6–41

Iturea and Trachonitis A.D. 34–37]

Herod Agrippa I (King)   Ituria and Trachonitis
                                                   A.D. 37–44

                                                   Galilee and Perea
                                                   A.D. 39–44

                                                   Judea and Samaria
                                                   A.D. 41–44

[Roman Procurators controlled Judea and Samaria A.D. 44 to 66/70;
Galilee and Perea A.D. 44–61 and 56; and Ituria and Trachonitis A.D. 44–53]

Herod Agrippa II (Tetrarch [later King])   Ituria and Trachonitis
                                                   A.D. 53–66

                                                   Galilee and Perea
                                                   A.D. 61 and 56–66

TABLE 4.3

A SUMMARY OF IMPORTANT DATES IN ISRAEL

Patriarchal Period
   Middle Bronze Age   ca. 2000ff. B.C.
The Exodus
   Last part of the Late Bronze Age   ca. 1280 B.C.
Reigns of David and Solomon
   and Building of First Temple
   (Transition from the Early Iron Age
   to the Middle Iron Age   ca. 1000–950 B.C.

Assyrian Conquest of Israel (The Northern Kingdom)	722 B.C.
Babylonian Conquest of Judah, Destruction of the First Temple and Exile to Babylon	587/586 B.C.
Cyrus Permits the Exiles to Return	539 B.C.
Dedication of the Second Temple	520/519 B.C.
Alexander defeats the Persians and conquers Syria, Palestine and Egypt	331 B.C.
The Ptolemies and Seleucids fight repeatedly for control of Palestine	323–142 B.C.
The Maccabean (Hasmonean) Rule	142–63 B.C.
Arrival of Pompey and the Romans	63 B.C.
The Rule of Herod the Great	(40) 37–4 B.C.
Rebuilding of the Second Temple (The Herodian Temple)	20/19 B.C.–A.D. 63
The Birth of Jesus	7–4 B.C.
The Ministry of Jesus	A.D. 27–28
The Jewish Rebellion	A.D. 66–72
The Fall of Jerusalem and Destruction of the Second Temple	A.D. 70
The *Bar Kokhba* Revolt	A.D. 132–135
The Beginning of the Byzantine Period, Founding of Constantinople and the Arrival of Helena in Palestine	A.D. 324–325
The Beginning of the Islamic Period	A.D. 636
The First Crusader Period	A.D. 1099–1187
Saladin's Victory over the Crusaders	A.D. 1187–1189
The Second and Third Crusader Period	A.D. 1190–1291
The Mameluke Victory and the end of the Crusades	A.D. 1290
The Ottoman Period	A.D. 1519–1917
The British Mandate	A.D. 1917–1947/1948

The Formation of the State of Israel
and the Conflict with the Palestinians   A.D. 1948–Present

V

VISITING THE NORTH IN ISRAEL

T HE NORTH IS USUALLY regarded as lying west of the Jordan River (modern Syria and Jordan [ancient Gilead]), north of the area assigned to Judah among the Israelite tribes and south of modern Lebanon and some of Mt Hermon, including the area which was resettled by the tribe of Dan. It formed the area called "Israel" in the divided kingdom (excluding Gilead). While this territory included the region of Samaria, most study tours today do not normally include this region which has been assigned to the Palestinian Authority.

THE NORTH IN ISRAEL (see also Around the Sea of Galilee)

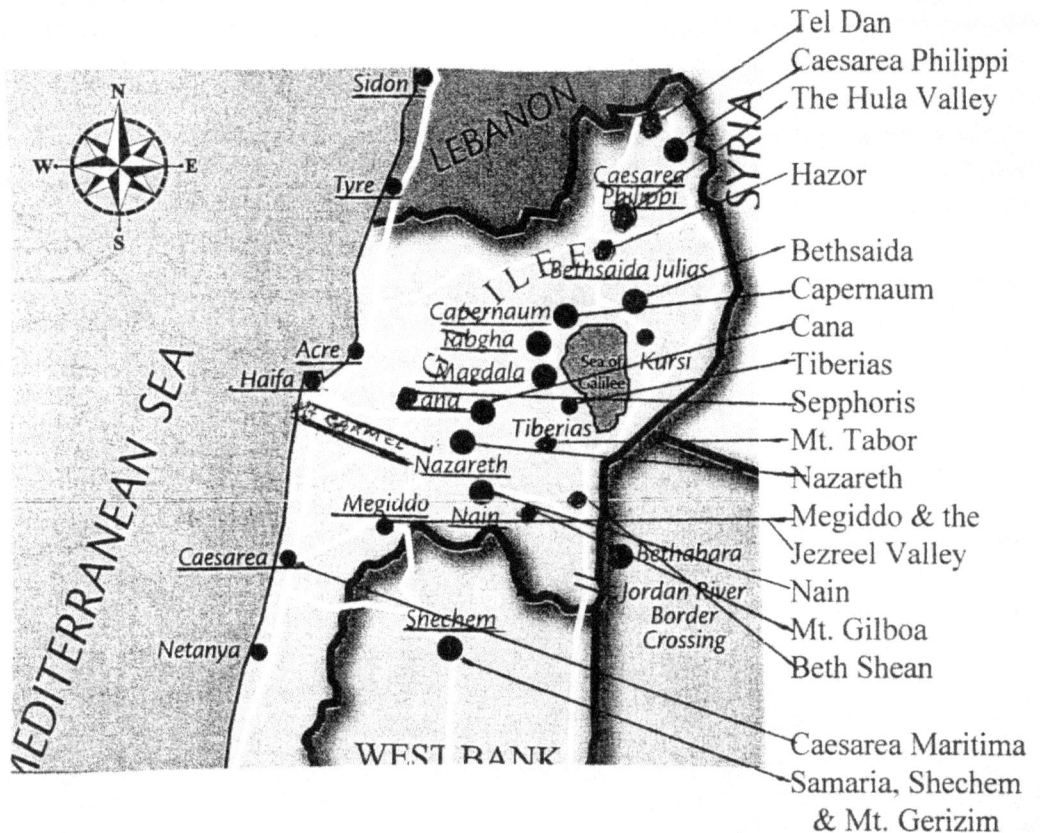

GALILEE

The word Galilee comes from the Hebrew *galilah*, which means circle or district, and denotes the territory in northern Palestine. The area appears in the Old Testament as "Galilee of the Gentiles/nations" (Isa 9:1; cf. Matt 4:5). It is this area which was the scene of Jesus's boyhood and his early ministry. After he began his ministry, his visited other places but Galilee was still regarded as his home (Matt 4:13). Most of his disciples were from Galilee, except Judas Iscariot (a Judean), and following his resurrection, Jesus made an appearance to his disciples in Galilee (Matt 28:7).

Galilee is an upland area which is bordered by plains including the Jezreel Valley in the south, by the Jordan Rift on the east, by the Mediterranean coast on the west and by rather high rolling hills on the north. It falls in two steps from the north. The higher step forms Upper Galilee, most of which is around 3,000 feet above sea level. In New Testament times it was a forested, thinly populated hill country with a broad swampy center area known as the Hula Valley, which has since been drained. The lower step forms Lower Galilee at from 1,500 to 2,000 feet above sea level but which falls steeply to around 600 feet below sea level at the Sea of Galilee.

Lower Galilee

It was in Lower Galilee where Jesus spent much of his ministry. Well-watered by streams which flowed from the northern hills, it contains large stretches of fertile land in the limestone basins among the hills. As a result, it is a region of dense, prosperous settlement from which olive oil, grain and fish from the lake were exported.

It was in this area encompassing limestone hills that Jesus grew up, a region traversed by several important imperial highways that meant the towns in that area were hardly backwater communities. Its agriculture, fisheries, and commerce provided Jesus with the cultural background that is reflected in many of his parables and other teachings. Its rather dense population for the time furnished Jesus and the disciples with a ready mission field. Records from that period suggest that there were about 200 villages near the Sea of Galilee, most of which have since disappeared.

Among the towns that existed in Lower Galilee during the time of Jesus only Nazareth, a "new Cana" along with Tiberias (which Jesus may not have visited) continues to flourish today. Important cities like Bethsaida, Sephoris, and Ch(K)orazin have ceased to exist.

Around the Sea of Galilee

AROUND THE SEA OF GALILEE

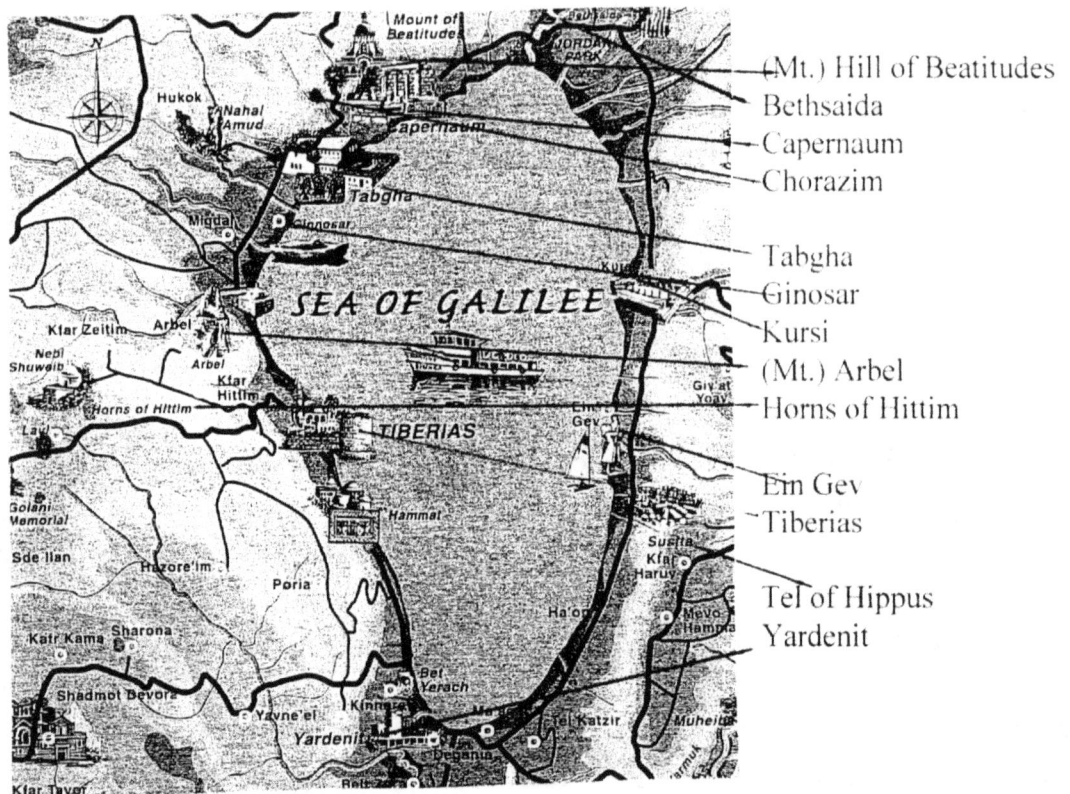

Capernaum, on the northwest side of the Sea of Galilee (Matt 4:12–14), is now basically only a Roman Catholic retreat center. The name is derived from the Hebrew *kephar nahum* which means "village of Nahum," but it is impossible to link it directly to Nahum the prophet. It is not mentioned in the Old Testament, probably because it was not established until after the exile. Jesus seems to have made his headquarters there, and it became known as "his home town" (Matt 9:1). In Jesus's day its importance as a divisional point or government center seems to be indicated by the presence of tax collectors like Matthew (Matt 9:9) and military officers such as a centurion (Matt 8:5–10). The actual extent of the city remains uncertain.

1. Ruins of the synagogue at Capernaum built over the earlier synagogue

The ruins of an extant third to fourth century white marble synagogue are built over what is judged to be an earlier black basalt synagogue (where Jesus probably spoke). Archaeologists have also uncovered a fifth century octagonal Byzantine church under which lies a fisherman's quarters, which may be associated with Peter and his mother-in-law (Mark 1:29–31).

On the southwest shore of the Sea of Galilee stands **Tiberias**, built by Herod Antipas in A.D. 18 and named after his Imperial patron. It was well known for its Roman baths supplied by hot sulphur springs. The baths were visited—and still are today—by many seeking refreshment or healing from ailments. In the fourth century, the Jews established an important rabbinic learning center at Tiberias, and here the Jerusalem Talmud was assembled. It was also here that the symbols for the vowels in the Hebrew alphabet were developed to assist in the reading of the ancient texts. About two and one-half miles north of Tiberias is the small settlement of Migdal, which preserves the ancient location of **Magdala** (Matt 15:39–40 and 27:56). Above the town stands the high mountain ridge known as the Arbel, where Josephus tells us the enemies of Herod the Great hid in caves after rebelling against him and whom he killed by having boiling oil and hot water poured from above through the crevasses in the mountain.

To the north of the Sea of Galilee lie the ruins of **Chorazin/Korazin** (Matt 11:21–23; Luke 10:13–15) that contain a black basalt synagogue dating from about A.D. 200. Nearby, on the shore of the sea, west of Capernaum is the important traditional fourth century chapel of **Tabgha** (from the Greek word *heptapegon*, "seven wells") which commemorates the **feeding of the five thousand** (John 6:1–14).

Above the north shore of the Sea of Galilee stands the beautiful octagonal **Church of the Beatitudes** commissioned by Mussolini and designed by Antonio Barluzzi on the sight which Egeria in her pilgrimage to the Holy Land had identified as the traditional site for the Sermon on the Mount by Jesus recorded in Matthew 5–7. The hillside below the Church would offer a convenient and picturesque place for speaking to a large crowd of people. East of this church and near the northern tip of the Sea of Galilee close to where the Jordan River enters the lake lie the ruins of what is believed to be the city of **Bethsaida** (either Khirbet el-Araj or Et-Tell).

The **Sea of Galilee** is a segment of Jordan Rift that belongs to the Pan-African fault. It is a small but deep lake approximately thirteen miles north to south and eight miles east to west at their longest points. Lying in a bowl surrounded by the Galilean hills on the west and the Golan Heights on the east, it is subject to powerful windstorms which come from the northwest through the Valley of the Pigeons and which at times stir the waters into drenching waves, reminding us of the storms on the Sea of Galilee in the stories of Jesus. Just west of Tabgha is the **Kibbutz Ginosar** where nearby residents found the so-called "**Jesus boat**" in 1986 stuck in the muddy shallows when the sea was unusually low. The boat is about 2,000 years old and measures nine meters (ca. twenty-nine feet) long by two and one-half meters (ca. seven feet) wide and one and one-quarter meters (four feet) high. It was carefully raised, and because the wood was badly deteriorated, it had to be reconstituted. It is now on display and provides some idea of how perilous it would have been to fish in such a small vessel during a **fierce storm** (Mark 4:35–41 and 6:45–52).

On the east side of the sea and below the Golan Heights is located Gergesa, or **Kursi**, the traditional site for the healing of the **Gadarene demoniac** and the drowning of the large herd of swine (Matt 8:28–34 and Luke 8:26–39). As I will indicate later in the section on Gadara in Jordan, this site is currently under **dispute**, and **readers should consult** that section for the way scholars try to confirm sites. South of Kursi is the hill and Tel of Hippus, one of the ten independent Greek cities (**Decapolis**), which Jesus probably visited (Mark 5:20 and 7:31). Near to Hippus is the modern Kibbutz Ein Gev, which is one of the places where visitors to Israel enjoy a meal of "**St. Peter's Fish**" as they dine overlooking the Sea of Galilee.

The Jordan and Beth Shan

At the south end of Sea of Galilee where the Jordan River makes its exit and meanders to the Dead Sea, a baptismal park has been constructed at Yardenit where pilgrims may be **baptized in the Jordan River** or reconfirm their baptisms while watching others being baptized. The actual place where Jesus was baptized by John the Baptist (Mark 1:9–11 and John 1:28) is much farther south in the desert near the Dead Sea but the river there today is rather contaminated.

2. Ruins of the Roman city of Beth Shan with the earlier tel in the background

South of the Sea of Galilee on a major branch of the *Via Maris* lies the historic city of **Beth Shan** (**Beit Shean**), the only city of the Decapolis on the west side of the Jordan. In Hellenistic times it was known as **Scythopolis**. Settlement began on the site as early as the fifth millennium B.C. After the defeat of **Saul and his sons** at Mt. Gilboa, the Philistines hung their beheaded bodies on the wall of the ancient city as a sign of desecration (1 Sam 31:8–10). The city was destroyed by the Assyrians in 732 B.C. but was typically rebuilt, and in the second century B.C. it was captured by the Hasmoneans, who exiled the Gentile inhabitants and resettled it with Jews. In the early stages of the war with the Romans (A.D. 66) the Gentiles killed the Jews in the city. The later grand Hellenistic city was not built on the Tel but in the valley below with wide colonnade streets, a theater seating 7,000, a great bathhouse, scores of shops, a Roman Temple, and a beautiful Nymphaeum (fountain dedicated to nymphs). For students of the Bible this site provides excellent insights into the contrast between an earlier Israelite city and its Hellenistic successor.

Central Galilee and the Jezreel Valley

To the west near the Central Ridge Road (Way of the Patriarchs) and in a high valley among the most southern limestone hills of the Lebanese range lies **Nazareth**, which in the time of Jesus was a small village but today is one of the larger cities of Israel. The town is not mentioned in the Old Testament or other early sources. Even though it lay close to several caravan routes, it was more of an independent frontier town that evoked some scorn by strict Jews (John 1:46). The name of the town is derived from the Aramaic *nas' rat, which* means "watch tower," suggesting that it might have been a military outpost. Here, Jesus grew not only in stature but also in favor with God and other people (Luke 2:52 and 4:16). Here in the **synagogue**, he announced his mission as the fulfillment of **God's Jubilee** (Luke 4:17–21). Here, the people also considered he had violated his station in life and sought to kill him by trying to throw him over the **precipice** (Luke 4:25–30). The city has expanded greatly so that not much remains of the ancient town, but the most authentic sites are the city well, which from the twelfth century A.D. has been known as "**Mary's Well**," located in the St. Gabriel's Greek Orthodox Church. Recently, archaeologists uncovered the remains of a home dating from about the time of Jesus. The traditional Church of the Annunciation is also located here. The Baptist Church of Nazareth near Mary's Well has a large school that educates many Christian and Muslim children. Visiting the small, reconstructed Nazareth Village is a special experience for those who have time. In this city Jesus became a **builder**. The Greek word *ho tekton* (Mark 6:3 and Matt 13:55) has been rendered "carpenter" for centuries, but it can mean various types of builders. Seeing all the stone buildings in Israel, one might wonder just a little if Jesus and Joseph might have had a broader trade.

The nearby large city in the region during the time of Jesus was **Sephoris/Zippori** (meaning "perched on a mountain like a bird"), which today lies in ruins. In 55 B.C., Gabinius, the Roman governor of Syria, declared Sephoris the capital of Galilee. **Herod the Great** started his political career here as the Governor of Galilee. The city undoubtedly employed **many artisans**, and Jesus may have found work in that city. Archaeologists have uncovered colonnaded streets, a theater seating about 4,000, and magnificent mosaic floors (which are on display), indicating that the residents of the city were quite wealthy. One of the floors on the crest of the hill contains a beautiful mosaic representing a U-shaped triclinium carpet meant to enhance a low table for the reclining dinner practice of the ancients (probably the kind employed at the last supper of Jesus). Some **traditions** indicate that the grandparents of Jesus might have lived in this city. During the Jewish uprisings against the Romans, the citizens of this city refused to join in the fighting, and as a result the Romans showered them with economic prosperity. The Jewish Mishnah reached its codified form here at the end of second century A.D. Later the Christians made Sephoris a bishopric and in the **Crusader** period many of the knights in full armor rode out from here on their disastrous journey to face the powerful Saladin at the **Horns of Hattin in 1187.**

Much earlier, to the south of Sephoris and Nazareth in the time of **Deborah**, the men of Zebulun and Naphtali, who had assembled on Mt. Tabor, defeated the Canaanite commander Sisera in the **Jezreel Valley** near **Mt. Tabor** when the Israelites chased the Canaanite forces all the way to *Harosheth hagoim* in the foothills near Mt. Carmel after God sent rain and hail so that the chariots became stuck in the mud. Then Jael dispatched the sleeping Sisera with a tent peg (Judg 4:4–22). Mostly because of convenience, traditions arose suggesting that Mt. Tabor was the place of the **Transfiguration**, but the more likely place is Mt. Hermon in northern Galilee (Mark 9:2–8).

Other sites of importance in this region include: (1) **Cana** (just north of Nazareth), where Jesus turned water into wine (John 2:1–11). The site of the original town is not entirely certain; however, it is remembered in the current nearby town of Kfar Kana. (2) **Nain** (just south of Nazareth and two miles from Mt. Tabor) is where Jesus raised the widow's son (Luke 7:11), and (3) **En Dor** (four miles south of Mt. Tabor) is where Saul consulted the witch or medium (1 Sam 28:7; for other incidents, cf. Josh 17:11 and Ps 83:10). (4) **Mt. Gilboa**, where Saul and Jonathan were killed (1 Sam 31:8), lies to the south of Nain and six miles west of Beth Shan. Near Mt. Gilboa lies (5) the **Spring of Harod** (Ein Harod), where God tested **Gideon**, whose army was reduced to a mere 300 men before doing battle with the Midianites (Judg 7:1–7).

Protecting the entrance to the Jezreel Valley from the south stands the Carmel mountain ridge, which is broken by two small passes and a larger one. Near Mt. Gilboa in the **Dothan Valley** is one of the **minor passes** in the mountain ridge through which runs the ancient ridge road, also know as the Way of the Patriarchs. The modern city of Jenin, ancient Beth Haggan, lies in this valley. Here in his search for his brothers, **Joseph** was seized and traded for "twenty silver coins" to Midianite merchants who carried him off and sold him as a slave in Egypt (Gen 37:25–29). In this valley, Jehu also shot (with an arrow) **Ahaziah**, the King of Judah, who died in nearby Megiddo (2 Kgs 9:27–28).

Guarding the largest pass on the *Via Maris* (the trunk road between Egypt and Mesopotamia) sits **Megiddo, one of the most famous cities of antiquity**, situated sixteen miles southeast of the modern seaport city of Haifa (the successor to the ancient seaport of **Acco**, which lies to the northwest; Judg 1:31). According to 1 Kings 9:15, **Solomon fortified three cities** on the *Via Maris*: **Gezer** in the south, to meet the forces of Egypt; **Megiddo**, to protect the center of the country from either direction; and **Hazor** in the north, to dispatch the armies from Mesopotamia.

3. Ruins of Tel Megiddo with the Canaanite worship center in the foreground

The fortress of **Tel Megiddo** dates back at least to 3500 B.C., and Thutmose III of Egypt—who captured it in 1468 B.C.—considered it to be worth "a thousand cities" (cf. biblical references in Josh 12:21, 17:11, and Judg 1:27). The tel has witnessed more than twenty habitations and destructions. Archaeologists have uncovered an early Canaanite altar, the remains of buildings, stables, grain storage facilities, and stone troughs for horses (all of which can be viewed at the site). They have even found flint tools and stone weapons from the Neolithic period.

Solomon apparently stationed many of his fourteen hundred chariots and twelve thousand horses at Megiddo (1 Kgs 10:26). The remains of the six-chambered gate found at the site may be identified with building styles from the Solomonic period. Ahab further enlarged the facilities by strengthening the gate and the walls and developed it into a "siege city" (a secured site that had a large storage system for supplies and constant access to water). The date of the tunnel that carried the water inside the city from the nearby spring, the source of which was then covered over and hidden, is not certain. Visitors find descending about 120 feet through the water system to be a fascinating venture. **Josiah**, the reformer and last of the great Davidic kings, lost his life at Megiddo to the forces of Pharaoh Neco (2 Kgs 23:28–30). Because of the bloody history connected with Megiddo, it became the **symbol of the final war** between the forces of God and the forces of Satan in the book of Revelation. It is known as **Armageddon** (Rev 16:16), from the Aramaic/Hebrew *har megiddo* ("the mountain of Megiddo").

Near the Mediterranean coast on the summit of **Mt. Carmel** stands a memorial to a decisive biblical confrontation between **Elijah** and the priests of Baal and Asherah. The question to be decided was: "Who is *El* (God)?" Was it *Baal* or *Yawheh?* Who would rain down fire and consume the sacrifice? The story in 1 Kings 18:17–39 is one that should send shivers to any human who thinks that God is helpless. The Kishon Brook at the foot of Mt. Carmel bore testimony to the victor as the people slaughtered those royal priests of **Jezebel**, Ahab's wife (1 Kgs 16:30–31 and 18:40). From this summit on Mt. Carmel, the visitor can receive a great view of the Jezreel Valley and the surrounding country on a clear day.

The Mediterranean Coast

Perhaps the most impressive city in the time of Jesus was **Caesarea Maritima**, built by Herod the Great as an exhibit of his greatness to the world. Anyone who has spent time digging in the city will agree that much more is still left to be uncovered, but in recent years much of the public area has emerged from the sands. To illustrate his vision, Herod built a gigantic harbor with a great 400-meter breakwater and a shorter breakwater to close in the harbor so that it would handle a huge fleet of ships. He built it in an area where there had been a small Phoenician village that later was called Straton's Tower, where only a small natural harbor had existed and the currents were very strong. In order to accomplish his dream, his engineers developed a cement that hardened underwater. Even today, the feat of his harbor construction amazes the contemporary mind. For example, to test the current strength, Israeli scientists dumped a very large rock into the Mediterranean near the harbor, and it soon disappeared from the area.

4. The elevated aqueduct at Caesarea Maritima (near the sea)

Herod's city took about twelve years to build, and it was finished by 9 B.C., about five years before his death. His palace, which faced out on the Mediterranean, must have been a marvel that left his visitors gasping at its magnificence. It contained grand meeting rooms, a double swimming pool, and all the amenities of sheer luxury. But remember that there was virtually no fresh water on the barren coast, so an elevated aqueduct was constructed to bring fresh water from the Carmel springs eight miles away. This necessitated the tunneling of a channel through the mountain ridge to carry the water. A lower aqueduct that brought water from the river about four miles away was also built.

But entertainment was very important to Herod. An impressive theater that could seat at least 4,000 was constructed, and it remained in use for hundreds of years after it was built. The stage contained a magnificent backdrop three stories in height for the scenery, and the orchestra was lavish in its marble-like flooring. Nearby was the magnificent amphitheater that seated about 10,000 spectators for racing and other special events. To add to the excitement, a great hippodrome seating 30,000 people was added to the facilities in the second century. The city was a favorite place for the political and military elite from Rome who were stationed in this section of the Mediterranean world.

Indeed, during the time I was teaching in Israel, the archaeological team uncovered at Caesarea the only **Mithraeum** found in Palestine. In order to protect its fragile elements, it was necessary to rebury it; however, it was reopened for inspection twenty-five years later when one of my doctoral students was also doing work at Caesarea. Despite our understanding of some of the mythological and astrological features of Mithra, there is much that we still do not know. We are aware that because of its emphasis on physical courage it was probably the favorite religion of the Roman military, and in many parts of the Roman Empire it vied with Christianity to become the faith of the people.

It is unlikely that Jesus visited Caesarea Maritima, but Acts mentions that **Philip** came to Caesarea (Acts 8:40), and **Peter** was instrumental in evangelizing Cornelius and the Gentiles there (10:1–11:18). After **Paul** became a Christian, it is evident that he certainly became familiar with the city (9:30; 18:22; and 21:8–16), because he was escorted under armed guard from Jerusalem and brought to Caesarea (23:23–24); that he was **imprisoned** there under the **procurators Felix and Festus** for about two years (23:24–25:27); that he appeared before **Herod Agrippa II** when he pled his case (26:1–31); and since he had **appealed to Caesar**, he was finally dispatched to Rome under guard from there (26:32–27:2).

Before leaving this area of the coast, it should be noted that sheltered from the strong southern current of the Mediterranean and north of the Carmel Peninsula lies the modern seaport city of **Haifa** (where Crusaders made their temporary headquarters in A.D. 1100). It has since replaced in importance the ancient harbor city of **Acco**, or **Ptolemais** (named after the Ptolemies, the successors of Alexander in Egypt), which is a short distance to the north (Judg 1:31 and Acts 21:7).

Hazor and the Hula Valley

Journeying north from the Sea of Galilee on the northern extension of the *Via Maris*, the traveler encounters historic **Tel Hazor**, which Solomon fortified to protect Israel from the northern invaders (1 Kgs 9:15). The tel is huge by most standards, and today the remains are on both sides of the modern highway. Not much is known about the city before the Middle Bronze Age, but by the end of that period (ca. 1600 B.C.) records indicate that it had become a **major city** and swelled to about 15,000 inhabitants who occupied both the upper and lower parts of the tel. Hazor served as the major city on the highway between **Damascus** (frequently mentioned in the Bible), the capital of both ancient Aram and modern Syria about fifty miles away and its seaport of **Acco** (Judg 1:31) Acre, or Ptolemais.

Under the leadership of Jaban, the King of Hazor, the Canaanite confederacy sought to stop the Israelite conquest of the land, but **Joshua** prevailed and **burned Hazor** in the Israelite practice of "devoting" the city to the Lord (Josh 11:1–15). The tel then stood vacant for more than a hundred years. But in the eleventh century B.C., parts of the upper city were resettled, and both Solomon and Ahab developed the city into a strong fortification that never expanded to the size of the earlier Canaanite city. The Assyrians under Tiglath-pileser III destroyed it in 732 B.C., along with other cities of the Northern Kingdom (Israel). Although there was some habitation in Hellenistic times, the Romans did not use it much. It stands today uninhabited as a mute testimony to a more significant past. Archaeologists continue to excavate the site.

Tel Hazor is located at the southern end of the **Hula Valley**, which before recent times was a swampy area that was mosquito infested; however, the swampy lake served as an important filter for the upper Jordan River as it made its way down to the Sea of Galilee. The modern Israelis drained the swamps to reduce the mosquito problem and to provide for more fertile land. Nevertheless, several unforeseen problems occurred, reminding us that care must be taken in tampering with aspects of natural conditions. One is that the filtering system for the Sea of Galilee was changed; a second is that the soil is less nutritious than anticipated; and the third is that the Hula swamp provided a convenient stopping place for birds on the European flyway during their annual migrations both north and south. Efforts are now being made to correct these imbalances.

Tel Dan and Caesarea Philippi

At the northern edge of modern Israel near one of the sources of the Jordan River lies **Tel Dan** (ancient Laish). Archaeologists have uncovered one of the two ancient worship sites (high places) that were set up by **Jeroboam I** (son of Nebat) when the northern tribes refused to pay the heavy taxes demanded by Rehoboam, the successor to Solomon (1 Kgs 12:1–15). After Jeroboam became the ruler of the Northern Kingdom, he purposely sought to redirect the worship patterns of Israel away from both the Temple in

5. *The Canaanite brick gate at Tel Dan*

Jerusalem and loyalty to the Davidic dynasty by establishing golden calves as the worship seats (thrones) for their "god" (1 Kgs 12:25–33). An inscription was found here from the later Hellenistic period that reads "to the god who is in Dan."

Whereas artifacts that have been uncovered at the site date from the latter part of the Neolithic Period, effective settlement began here in the early Bronze Period (ca. 2500 B.C.). Remains of an earthen wall (glacis) have been found that encircled the town and was probably encountered by the Danites when they came north to seize the city (Judg 18:27–29). In the beautiful fifty-acre nature preserve that represented ancient Dan, archeologists have recently discovered an impressive **Canaanite city brick gate**, which was undoubtedly in existence at the time when Abraham entered the land of Canaan. A short distance away, archaeologists also uncovered the well-preserved **Israelite stone gate**, which includes the bench where the city elders would have conducted their business. Among other significant finds at Dan was a ninth century fragmentary inscription in which the king of Damascus proclaims his victory over the king of Israel and the king of the **House of David**. The proclamation is important because one must remember that David conquered Damascus, forcing the citizens to pay him tribute (2 Sam 8:6) and that Hadadezer had been a harassing thorn during Solomon's reign (1 Kgs 11:23–25). But more important is the fact that this tablet represents the first archaeological discovery that directly mentions the name of "David." Dan remained inhabited until the Roman period when Paneas (or Banias)—later Caesarea Philippi—became the capital of the north.

Not far from Tel Dan lie the ruins of the Roman city of **Paneas**. The Arabic-speaking residents had difficulty pronouncing the "P," so the name became "**Banias**." Here was constructed an elaborate Paneon, a temple to the Greek god Pan in front of the great cave marking the dwelling of Pan. When the Romans took control of the area, they added it to the domain of Herod the Great. Adjacent to the Paneon and nearby springs which flow from Mt. Hermon and are one of the three sources of the **Jordan River**, Herod built a beautiful temple and dedicated it to Augustus, his imperial patron (after the demise of Mark Antony). Following Herod's death, this region was bestowed on one of his sons, Herod Philip, who made it his capital and renamed the city **Caesarea Philippi**. When Herod Agrippa II, who questioned Paul at Caesarea (Acts 26:1–32), assumed authority for the territory, he expanded and refurbished the city.

Jesus made a significant journey to this city during his lifetime, and it was here that he asked his disciples: "Who do people say that I am?" The people and the disciples were confused, and suggestions were made that he was a kind of reincarnation of an earlier prophet or John the Baptist. But when Jesus probed who the disciples thought he was, Peter responded that Jesus was, "**Christ, the Son of the living God.**" Although Peter was certainly correct and was clearly commended as blessed by Jesus for his confession, he really did not understand what he had said and soon faced a condemnation of being joined to Satan as well (Matt 16:13–23). Probably gazing at this religious site, the Paneon with its huge cave, also evoked from Jesus a prediction that the Gates of Hades (or the realm of the dead and pseudo gods) could not stand against the **Great Stone** that was being rejected. Traditions concerning Simon that identify "Peter" (a kind of nickname like "Rocky") with the Great Stone are misdirected, since 1 Peter 1:4–8 reminds Christian readers to come to the "living stone," the "corner stone," the "rejected stone" (Jesus) and become copies, or "living stones," themselves.

Nearby, probably on **Mt. Hermon** (Mark 9:2–13), Jesus provided an unforgettable experience to three of his disciples during his **Transfiguration**, when he spoke with Moses and Elijah in preparation for his "departure" (the Greek is *exodos*; cf. Luke 9:31) from this world. When Peter in his enthusiasm tried to link Jesus with the two great figures of the Old Testament, he was reminded by a dark cloud and the voice of God that such a linkage was totally inappropriate.

SAMARIA

Unfortunately at the present time, most pilgrims to the lands of the Bible are not scheduled to visit most sites in Samaria because of the political situation, but for the sake of completeness a brief discussion is included here by the author who has traveled in this area a number of times.

The Vicinity of the City of Samaria

Samaria was the name assigned to the **region** that, during the time of Jesus, lay between Judea in the south and Galilee in the north. It was also the name of the **ancient city** that became the capital of the Northern Kingdom in 925 B.C. when Omri was the sixth king of Israel. It was situated about forty-two miles north of Jerusalem, but unlike Jerusalem, which lies tucked in the mountains, Samaria was easier to attack because it was closer to the *Via Maris* and invading forces with their chariots. It fell to the conquering Assyrian forces of Shalmaneser V in 722 B.C., and many of its people were carried off into other lands controlled by Assyria. In their place, Gentiles from other conquered lands were settled here. The leaders of the exiled Jews who returned from Babylon rejected the mixture of the population thus created. The Samaritans in turn became fierce opponents of the Jews in their rebuilding efforts. Also condemned were the remnants of the Jews who had been left in Judea by Babylonians but who had entered mixed marriages (Ezra 4:1–4 and 9:1–10:17; Neh 2:19–20; etc.).

The Hasmonean John Hyrcanus later destroyed Samaria in 128 B.C. and dealt forcefully with the Samaritans, thus increasing the hostility. Following the securing of his position in the land, Herod the Great rebuilt a portion of the site as a fortress city and called it **Sebaste** (from the Greek *sebō* "I worship") in order to honor his imperial patron, Augustus. A few pillars and some other ruins remain at the site today. The hostility between the Jews and the Samaritans continued in the days of Jesus as witnessed in the words of the Samaritan woman who reflected that "the Jews have no dealings with the Samaritans" (John 4:9). But Jesus treated the Samaritans differently, and they responded by calling him "the Savior of the world" (4:39–42). He even told a parable that represented a Samaritan as a kind and generous hero, at the same time picturing the Jewish religious elite as uncaring humans (Luke 10:25–37).

Among the intriguing facts concerning the Samaritans is their retention of the **Samaritan Pentateuch** as their holy book but as an edited version of the Torah to fit their situation. It was clearly rejected by the Jews. The opportunity to witness a **Samaritan Passover celebration** on **Mt. Gerazim**, conducted by the few Samaritans who still survive, is an experience to remember. The lambs are killed, and the blood is sprinkled on the men and boys while they chant their songs to their Lord. It reminds one of a synthesis of going to a rock concert and visiting a slaughterhouse at the same time. One cannot help but recall the words of Jesus to the **Samaritan woman** when he said, "You worship what you do not know" (John 4:22). Of course, such words in our politically correct generation would hardly be acceptable to many.

Six miles northwest of Samaria and nineteen miles east of the Mediterranean Sea is the ancient city of **Shechem.** Here, Abraham stopped at the "oak of Moreh," and God promised that his descendants would inherit the land (Gen 12:6–7). Shechem was one of the "cities of refuge" to which those suspected of crimes could flee in order to have a fair trial (Josh 20:7). The story of the Samaritan woman also takes place at nearby **Sychar** at a well that was attributed to the patriarch Jacob. The site was earlier identified by some with Askar, but excavations at Balatah between Mt. Ebal and Mt. Gerazim, which is fairly close to the well, have identified the site with ancient **Shechem**, which **Abraham** visited on his way from Haran (Gen 12:5–6) and where **Jacob** camped after meeting with Esau (Gen 33:18–20). Here, **Joshua** gathered the tribes for his farewell address (Josh 24:1), and here it was that **Rehoboam** was installed as king after the death of Solomon (1 Kgs 12:1). The Romans called the city Neapolis, and today the place is called Nablus, one of the chief cities of the Palestinian Authority.

Bethel, Ai, and the Beth Horon Pass

One of the most historic sites in the history of Israel is **Bethel** ("House of God"). Lying twelve miles north of Jerusalem and in the territory assigned to Benjamin, it was on the main route to ancient Shechem. Near here (between Bethel and Ai), **Abraham** pitched his tent for a period of time after he received the promise at Shechem that God would give his descendants the land (Gen 12:8). Here too, **Jacob**, on his flight from Beer Sheba and his brother Esau, lay down and in the night experienced a strategic vision (or dream) of a staircase (or ladder) on which the angels of God were ascending and descending. In that dream God also promised to give him and his descendants the land where he was sleeping. On rising, he anointed his stone pillow and called the place Bethel (Gen 28:10–22, 31:13, and 35:1–3).

Luz was likely the name of the original nearby town, and **Bethel** probably developed into the religious center (Gen 28:19, 35:6, and 48:3). Samuel also made it a place where legal decisions were given to the people (1 Sam 7:16). Here, **Jeroboam I** in an effort to protect his dynasty set up for Israel one of the two **golden calves** as an alternative worship center to Jerusalem (see also Dan) after the kingdom was divided (1 Kgs 12:29). This decision raised fierce condemnations from the prophets (Amos 3:13–14 and 5:4–5; Hos 10:14–15; and Jer 48:13).

The small town of **Ai** became a significant symbol for Israel concerning the results of disobeying God. After conquering the strong city of Jericho, the forces of Joshua were defeated here because Achan hid booty from Jericho and refused to devote the entire city to fire (Josh 7:1–26).

Finally, in this brief sketch of Israel's midsection, it is crucial to mention the **Upper Beth Horon Pass**. Anyone who has mounted the hill here recognizes immediately how strategic this site was in ancient times. From it, one can see the surrounding countryside and the great valley below. Plans for the defense of the upland from attack can be modified as one watches the approaching enemy's strategy. Here, the Israelites who lived in the hills beyond could hide in the caves and behind trees as the enemy struggled to mount the heights. Chariot forces, which were a powerful fighting weapon in the valley below at Lower Beth Horon, were hardly as effective on the narrow road that offered the important **northern access to Jerusalem.**

Instead of coming to Beth Horon from the west and the *Via Maris*—as **most of the invaders** did in the time of Israel's conquest of the land—**Joshua** entered the territory from Jericho and Ai and came down upon Lower Beth Horon from the east and from

6. An early wine press, perhaps like the one used by Gideon (Judg 6:11)

above. In this strategic battle for the land, the Lord sent down hailstones and gave Joshua strength and time to wipe out the enemy (Josh 10:1–14). **Solomon** later fortified both Upper and Lower Beth Horon in his goal of protecting center of the country (2 Chr 8:5).

VI

VISITING THE SOUTH IN ISRAEL

THE SOUTH IS USUALLY regarded as the territory comprising the southern part of Mediterranean coastal plain including the land of the Philistines, the lower hill country known as the Shephelah, the mountain ridge from Jerusalem south through Hebron to Beer Sheba, and the lower Jordan Valley including the desert plain and the Dead Sea. Besides the coastal land of the Philistines, it usually is regarded as the territories originally assigned to the tribes of Dan, Judah, and Simeon.

THE SOUTH IN ISRAEL

THE SOUTHERN COAST AND THE LOWER (The Shephelah)

Joppa and the Sharon Valley

Situated less than forty miles to the south of the great seaport of Caesarea Maritima is the ancient seaport of **Joppa** where Hiram, the King of Tyre, floated the lumber from Lebanon to Solomon for the building of the Jerusalem Temple (2 Chr 2:16). Here also is the place where Jonah embarked on a ship in his attempt to run away from the Lord (Jonah 1:3). Likewise, here is the place where **Peter** received his daytime vision of a sheet filled with what must have looked to him like a zoo, and he was instructed concerning a new perspective on kosher people like **Cornelius** and the Gentiles (Acts 10:5–28).

Today, Joppa is part of Israel's modern metropolis of **Tel Aviv-Yafo** (Jaffa), which is about eleven miles from Lod in the Sharon Valley where the **Ben-Gurion International Airport** is now located and visitors to Israel arrive and depart. Lod (also **Lydda**) is where Peter healed the bedridden Aeneas (Acts 9:32–35). The fertile **Sharon Valley** has been known from ancient times as a symbol of a beautiful and fruitful land (see the "Rose of Sharon" in Song 2:1). Isaiah likens Judah's broken condition to Sharon as a "desert" but her return from exile as the majesty of Carmel and Sharon in full blossom (Isa 33:9 and 35:2).

The Philistine Pentapolis and the Shephelah

After the failing to conquer Egypt, the Philistines settled in the coastal plain north of the Sinai by covenant with the victorious Egyptians, and from there they sought to conquer the rest of the Levant. Sometimes they were successful in their expansion goals, but then they were pushed back. Nevertheless, they remained a constant threat to the Is-raelites until David and Solomon curtailed their ambitions. Their **five major cities** from north to south along the coast were **Ashdod**, **Ashkelon**, and **Gaza** and inland, **Ekron** and **Gath** near the *Via Maris* (Josh 13:3 and Judg 3:3).

> **Note:** Visitors to Israel today should be aware that most pilgrimage tours to the Bible Lands do not include the **Gaza Strip** on their itineraries because of the instability there. Accord-

ingly, great care should be exercised before deciding to travel in that part of the ancient Philistine Pentapolis.

During the **period of the judges**, the Israelites were unable to subdue the people in the land and indeed were constantly tempted to follow their ways, and in the pattern of syncretism they adopted both the gods of their neighbors as well as the Lord (Yahweh). The judges—or periodic commanders—of Israel like Gideon and Jephthah arose to defeat Israel's enemies and return them to revere Yahweh; a clear commitment to the God of Abraham, however, did not seem to last very long, and the people soon returned to do what was "right in their own eyes" (Judg 31:25).

Some of their judges, like **Samson**, were not necessarily models of morality. Samson's feats of strength in harassing the Philistines are well known; nevertheless, he ultimately fell to the sexual wiles of Delilah from Gaza, and he finally died a blind man when he destroyed the **Temple of Dagon in Gaza** (Judg 16:1–30).

At the close of the period of the judges, Eli's sons thought they could use the **ark of covenant** to defeat the Philistines at **Aphek** in the Sharon plain, but Israel received a lesson that the God of Israel could not be used, and the Ark was captured.[1] After the **capture of the ark**, the Philistines placed it in the **Temple of Dagon** in **Ashdod**, but the statute of their god fell and was broken. The people also became afflicted with tumors (1 Sam 4:1–11 and 5:1–6). The rulers of the Philistines then tried to take the ark to **Gath** and **Ekron**, but in both places the people protested. So the priests of the Philistines ordered that **five** golden mice and **five** golden tumors be fashioned as a guilt offering and sent back to Israel through the Shephelah (hill country) to **Beth Shemish** (1 Sam 5:8–6:16).

The Philistines continued to plague **Saul**, the first king of Israel, and in the hill country at the **Valley of Elah** near **Azeka** they challenged the Israelites to bring forth their champion who would fight the Philistine giant **Goliath of Gath**, who was nearly ten feet tall. As is well-known, **David** entered the picture and killed Goliath with a sling (1 Sam 17:1–54). But Saul became increasingly jealous of David and sought to kill him. So for a time, **David lived among the Philistines** near Gath (27:3) but was later dismissed by the Philistines prior to their battle with the Israelites once again at **Aphek** (29:1–6). Then, as noted earlier, the Philistines in the north on Mt. Gilboa killed Saul and his sons, and their decapitated bodies were hung for public display on the wall of Beth Shan (31:8).

When David became king over all Israel and Judah, the Philistines launched an at-

---

1. Aphek was later known as the Roman fortress of **Antipatris** near the *Via Maris*, where Paul was rushed from Jerusalem in a midnight escape from his assassins (Acts 23:31).

tack on the Israelites in the **Rephaim Valley** north of Ekron and west of what was to become the city of David (Jerusalem). David decisively defeated them and began subduing Israel's enemies. This initial battle was concluded near the *Via Maris* and the strategic site of **Gezer** (2 Sam 5:17–25 and 8:1–14), which later became the southern defensive stronghold against attacks from Egypt and one of the three chariot cities that were fortified by **Solomon.**

For readers of the New Testament, it is important to remember that in the expansion of early Christianity **Philip** was sent to **Gaza**, where he evangelized the Ethiopian eunuch who had just come from worshiping in Jerusalem. Then, Luke indicates that before he preached in Caesarea Maritima among the Gentiles, Philip was found working in **Azotus**, which was the Greek name for the Philistine city of **Ashdod** (Acts 8:26–40).

South of Ekron and Gath and due east of Ashkelon in the **lower hills** stands the ancient **fortress city of Lachish**, which now lies in ruins. Lachish had a **long history** because in the caves below the tel, artifacts have been found dating back to the Chalcolithic period (ca. 3500 B.C.). The remains of houses that date to the Middle Bronze period have also been uncovered. The **Hyksos**, who took **control of Egypt** ca. 1730 B.C., made Lachish one of their fortress cities. While archaeological work has now ceased at the tel, what is clear at this point is that at the high place three temples were constructed one on top of the other, dating from the fifteenth, fourteenth, and thirteenth centuries B.C. The Hyksos were probably shepherd warriors and were likely the Pharaohs when **Joseph** was brought to Egypt.

The Israelites under **Joshua** conquered the city ca. 1222–1220 B.C. and killed all the inhabitants there (Josh 10:31–32). By the time of Solomon, it served as an important military outpost for the defense of Jerusalem against enemies who sought to enter the region through the passes that led up to Bethlehem. **Archaeologists** have found a **palace** that they have dated to the reign of Rehoboam (928–911 B.C.). Understanding its important strategic nature, Asa strengthened the **walls**, a section of which was found to be about eighteen feet thick. Also found was the **beginning of a shaft** to a water source that might have provided water and perhaps protected the city in the time of siege, but it was not completed. During his reign, **Hezekiah** experienced the fall of Samaria to the Assyrians under Shalmaneser (722 B.C.), and ten years later the **Assyrians** were back again under Sennacherib; this time they came to Judah and Lachish (2 Kgs 18:9–17). Jerusalem ultimately escaped, but the strategic fortress of **Lachish was conquered** (2 Chr 32:9–21 and Isa 36:1–3). Judah's strategic fortress fell again with the invasion of the **Babylonians** under Nebuchadnezzar before the fall of Jerusalem (Jer 34:7).

JERUSALEM AND ITS ENVIRONS[2]

Jerusalem: The City of Three Faiths

Jerusalem is a special place for the Jews, the Muslims, and the Christians. Visitors to the old city will experience the interesting phenomenon on Fridays, whereby some of the shops close for the Muslim day of worship; on Saturdays some of the shops close for the Jewish day of worship; and on Sundays some of the shops close for the Christian day of worship.

For the Jews, Jerusalem is the traditional site of a mountain in "Moriah," where it is believed that Abraham was about to sacrifice Isaac (Gen 22:2); the Jebusite city that the forces of David conquered by climbing the water shaft and the city which he chose to make his capital for the United Kingdom (2 Sam 5:1–9); the place of the threshing floor of Araunah that David purchased and where Solomon built the Temple (2 Sam 24:18–25 and 1 Kgs 5:1–6:38); the place that was destroyed by the Babylonians in 587–586 B.C. (2 Kgs 25:8–17) and was rebuilt by Ezra and Nehemiah; the place where Antiochus (IV) Epiphanes desecrated the Temple by killing a pig on the altar of sacrifice (Dan 11:31); and the place where Herod provided the funds for the beautiful reconstruction of the Second Temple (Mark 13:1). It is the place that the Jews today have made their capital for the state of Israel.

---

2. For an excellent resource on Jerusalem see Richard M. Mackowski, SJ, *Jerusalem: City of Jesus* (Grand Rapids: Eerdmans, 1980).

THE OLD CITY OF JERUSALEM TODAY

(© Copyright Gerald L. Borchert 1998)

For the Muslims, after capturing Jerusalem from the Christians, it is the place that they have insisted is the traditional place—contrary to the Jewish tradition—that Abraham attempted to sacrifice Ishmael; the place where they believe that Mohammad visited on his nocturnal visionary travels before ascending to heaven; where they believe there is a footprint of Mohammad in the stone; where Abd el Maik in A.D. 685-705 built the Dome of the Rock to commemorate the sacrifice of Ishmael; and where the silver-domed El Aqsa mosque is located. It is for Muslims the Third Holy City after Mecca and Medina and the place today where the Palestinians desire to have their capital of a country called Palestine.

For the Christians, it is significant because it is the place where the wise men (stargazers) came looking for the baby Jesus (Matt 2:2–3); where Jesus was brought as a baby for his typical Jewish ceremony of repurchase by an offering as the eldest male child (Luke 2:22–40); where as a youth he was probably brought for his ceremony of initiation into adulthood—a Bar Mitzvah (2:41–52); where he taught and where he was rejected (19:41–20:47); where he died by crucifixion (23:26–49); and where he was raised from the dead (24:1–11 and 24:36–48). For Christians, Jerusalem has also become a symbol of our future life with God in the New Jerusalem, the eschatological Holy City (Rev 21:1–3).

After Constantine became the Roman Emperor, the Queen Mother, Helena, came to Israel and sought to discover the sites associated with the life of Jesus. At her direction, Constantine's builders began construction of royal churches throughout the land, particularly in Jerusalem and Bethlehem. As noted in the work of Eusebius and in the mosaic in the church of St. Pudentiana in Rome, the churches in Jerusalem included the central Church of the Holy Sepulcher; the Church of Holy Sion (Zion); and across the Kidron Valley on the Mount of Olives, the Church of Eleona. The Persians in their conquest of Palestine severely damaged or destroyed most of them, except (as noted earlier) the Church of the Nativity in Bethlehem. The Church of the Holy Sepulcher has been reconstructed a number of times and remains today as a central site for pilgrims. Many other churches have since been constructed as pilgrimage sites in Jerusalem.

The Physical Features of Jerusalem and Their Importance

Jerusalem lies in the mountains, so the visitor to Jerusalem should always be prepared to wear a jacket in the evenings, especially if the wind is blowing. In the winter, snow is rare, but it can be witnessed in this area; although from my experiences, it seldom lasts for more than a few hours and melts when the sun reaches full strength.

Being in the mountains means that Jerusalem is built on hills and valleys, and the valleys run from north to south. Three valleys are important in the history of Jerusalem. They are from east to west: (1) the **Kidron Valley** (also called the Valley of Jehoshaphat, from the Hebrew meaning "God is Judge") in which is located the **Gihon Spring** (the water source for ancient Jerusalem). The Kidron lies between the Mount of Olives on the east and the **Ophel** (city of David) and Temple Mount (Mt. Moriah) on the west. (2) The **Tyropean Valley** (or Valley of the Cheese Makers) which runs through the center of the Old City from the meeting point of the three valleys in the south to the **Damascus Gate** in the north. It is located along the west side of the Ophel and the Temple Mount and on the east side of what came to be known as Mount Zion (Sion), the expanded city from the time of the Maccabees and Jesus. Finally, (3) the **Hinnom Valley** on the west side of the expanded city in the time of Jesus came to have negative connotations (as Gehenna) because of the earlier sacrifices of children to Moloch in this valley, and the valley at times served as a place for refuse.

Because the valleys met in the south and created cliffs, which could be rather easily defended, in its **history** the **enemies** of Jerusalem normally attacked from the **north**. The north was thus viewed as its vulnerable side. When the modern Israelis stormed the Old City in **1948**, they knew its history and that the Palestinian forces would have expected an attack from the north such as at the Damascus Gate, so they scaled the hill and attacked from the south west at the **Zion Gate**.

The Present Gates of Jerusalem, the Quarters (Sections) of the Old City, and Their Significant Sites

Because the old city can become confusing for visitors to Jerusalem, one of the most important tasks in orientation is to learn where the gates of Jerusalem are located. These gates lead into the various sections of the Old City that are usually called quarters, although the religious sites are spread throughout the sections of the city.

The Christian Quarter

For the visitor, we start at the western gate, which is (1) **the Jaffa Gate**[3]. Near this gate Herod the Great built his triple-towered fortress close to where the citadel and a police station are now situated. From the gate leading directly east is David Street, which juts a little and becomes Chain Street; that in turn leads directly to the Temple Mount, thus bisecting the city north and south. At the Jaffa Gate, visitors can find a taxi if they become lost from their guides.

To the north and near the northwestern corner of the Arabic walls of the city is (2) **The New Gate**, which is the entrance to the northern Christian Quarter of the city. Facing out on the street is where the Old Green line was drawn that earlier divided the city into East and West Jerusalem. Within this quarter is situated the **Church of the Holy Sepulcher**. The great domed structure is traditionally regarded as the place in which the last five stations of the *Via Dolorosa* are said to have occurred. The site was identified by Queen Helena and has had a long tradition supporting its choice. Today the Church is home to **various Orthodox and Roman Catholic chapels**, and the various groups share the sites that are said to represent the places of the Crucifixion and Tomb of Jesus. While teaching in Jerusalem, I witnessed **conflicts** over times for controlling access to the tomb and the receiving of donations. Any changes to the church, even for painting or repairing, require the agreement of all parties (which has virtually been impossible to obtain). But the church is finally in the process of being painted and redecorated because of the insistence of the Israeli authorities. Across the street from the Church of the Holy Sepulcher is the more recently built **Lutheran Church of the Redeemer**, under which archaeologists have sought to confirm with some modicum of success the position of the ancient wall of Herod's city.

---

3. I have numbered the gates on the Map of the Old City of Jerusalem.

The Muslim Quarter

East from the New Gate along the northern wall one reaches (3) **the beautiful Damascus Gate**, which faces on East Jerusalem, the old Palestinian section of town. The streets from the gate lead north to the **Garden Tomb**, the Albright Institute for Archaeological Research, and the old bus station, which is in front of the hill that is filled with cracks and holes that General Gordon thought looked like **Skull Hill** (Golgotha).

7. The cliff identified by General Gordon as Golgotha (Skull Hill)

South from the gate and within the Old City, a series of streets somewhat following the base of the **Tyropean Valley** bifurcate the city east and west and divide the Christian Quarter from the eastern Muslim Quarter.

East from the Damascus Gate is (4) **Herod's Gate**, which leads into East Jerusalem near the famous **Rockefeller Museum**, where much of the analysis was done on the Dead

Sea Scrolls. Entering the city at this point leads to the residences of the Muslim Quarter.

Turning south at the corner of the walled city, one soon reaches the entrance known as both (5) the **Lion's Gate** because of the small lions near the lintels, and **St. Stephen's Gate** because tradition indicates that it was from this gate that Stephen was dragged out of the city and stoned under the direction of the persecutor Saul/Paul (Acts 7:58). This gate faces east on the Mount of Olives. As one enters the city from the east, the **Temple Mount** is on the left hand side, and on the right one soon comes to the **Church of Saint Anne** (the mother of Mary), where visitors are usually awed by the magnificent acoustics as they sing in the church. In the same courtyard lie the ruins of the **Pool of Bethesda**, which had five porches and witnessed the healing by Jesus of the man who had been paralyzed for thirty-eight years and where a legend grew up attributing the periodic siphoning action of the water to the descent of an angel (John 5:2–15).

8. The original street level of the Tower of Antonio in the basement of the Sisters of Zion Convent

Following the street westward, the visitor soon comes to the convent of the **Sisters of Zion**, which is built over part of the site where the tall **Tower of Antonio** once stood. It was built by Herod the Great in order that the activities of the Jews could be closely observed and was named in honor of his first patron, Mark Antony. From this tower the Tribune quickly entered the Temple courtyard and **rescued Paul** when it was observed that he was being beaten in the Temple (Acts 21:32). But perhaps more significant is the experience that many pilgrims gain when they visualize that the flooring of one of the basement levels contains a portion of the **street level of the ancient fortress** where people and horses **walked** and the courtyard of the tower where **prisoners were whipped**. A game played by the soldiers was carved into the stonework and is still evident today. One tradition asserts that here is where Jesus was whipped before being crucified. An alternative view is that he was scourged at the triple tower fortress near the Jaffa Gate.

VIA DOLOROSA
THE FOURTEEN STATIONS OF THE CROSS

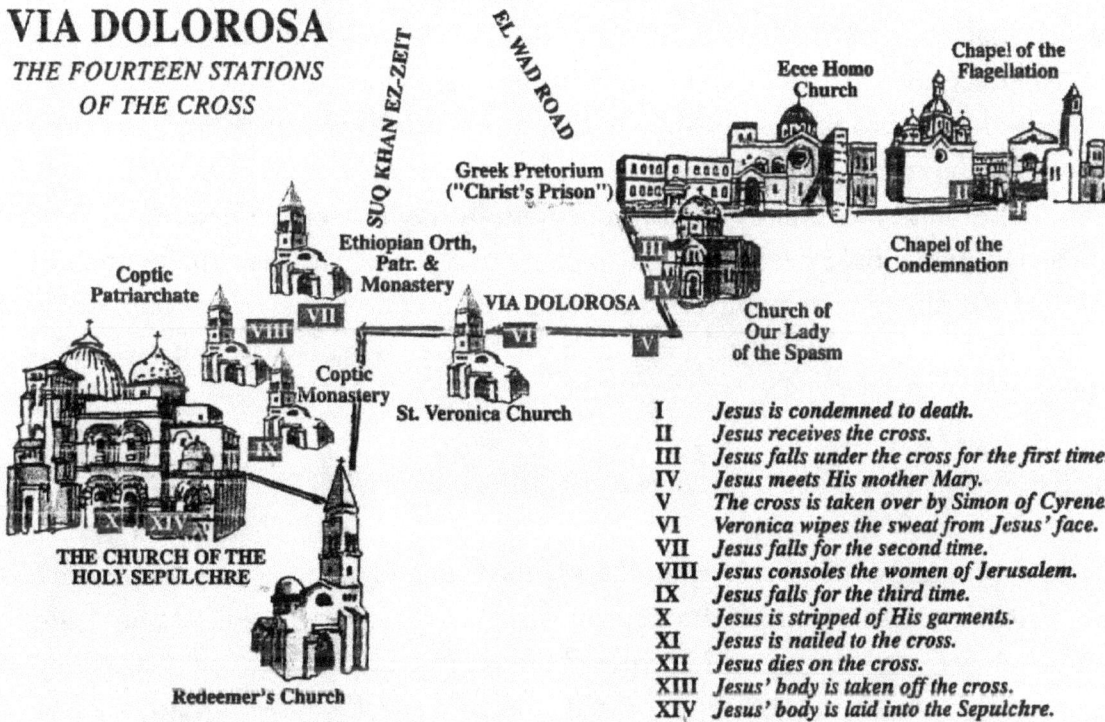

SUQ KHAN EZ-ZEIT

EL WAD ROAD

Ecce Homo Church

Chapel of the Flagellation

Greek Pretorium ("Christ's Prison")

Ethiopian Orth. Patr. & Monastery

Chapel of the Condemnation

Coptic Patriarchate

VIA DOLOROSA

Church of Our Lady of the Spasm

Coptic Monastery

St. Veronica Church

THE CHURCH OF THE HOLY SEPULCHRE

Redeemer's Church

I	*Jesus is condemned to death.*
II	*Jesus receives the cross.*
III	*Jesus falls under the cross for the first time.*
IV	*Jesus meets His mother Mary.*
V	*The cross is taken over by Simon of Cyrene.*
VI	*Veronica wipes the sweat from Jesus' face.*
VII	*Jesus falls for the second time.*
VIII	*Jesus consoles the women of Jerusalem.*
IX	*Jesus falls for the third time.*
X	*Jesus is stripped of His garments.*
XI	*Jesus is nailed to the cross.*
XII	*Jesus dies on the cross.*
XIII	*Jesus' body is taken off the cross.*
XIV	*Jesus' body is laid into the Sepulchre.*

Further west on the street is located the **Ecce Homo Arch**, the traditional site where Jesus was presented to the crowd with Pilate's words "**Behold the man**" (John 19:5). This site is very significant for many pilgrims to Jerusalem because it marks the **beginning of the Fourteen Stations of the *Via Dolorosa***, several of which are not mentioned in any of the Gospels but are traditional developments. Among these stations, there are nine that may be supported by scripture. They are: (1) Jesus was condemned to death; (2) the cross was placed on Jesus; (5) Simon was conscripted to carry the cross; (8) Jesus addressed the women about weeping; (10) Jesus was stripped of his clothing; (11) Jesus was nailed to the cross; (12) Jesus died; (13) Jesus was removed from the cross and prepared for burial; and (14) Jesus was placed in the tomb. From the tomb he arose on the first Easter Sunday morning in confirmation of his divinely appointed mission. The remaining five stations (some of which may be true but represent traditional developments by people of faith) are: (3) Jesus fell the first time; (4) Jesus met his mother; (8) Veronica wiped Jesus's face; (7) Jesus fell a second time; and (9) Jesus fell a third time.[4]

The next gate, (6) the **Golden Gate**, is sealed in the eastern wall, and a tradition has emerged that it will remain closed until the Messiah arrives. The **Muslims** have purposely established a **graveyard** along the eastern wall of Jerusalem for two reasons. The first is in order to be close to the important site that was visited by Muhammad, but the second is to render the coming of the **Messiah** impossible because they relate to the Jewish tradition that dead bodies make places and people **ritually unclean**. Therefore, it is believed that the Messiah would never attempt to come to a place that was ritually unclean.

The old Sheep Gate mentioned in John 5 no longer exists. Also nonexistent today are the Fountain Gate, the Water Gate, and the Horse Gate discussed in Nehemiah 3:15, 26, and 28.

The Temple Mount and the Overlap of the Muslim and Jewish Quarters

In the middle of the southern wall is (7) the **Dung Gate**, which is west of the **Earlier Main Entrance** to the **Temple**, the steps of which have recently been excavated and today are just below the silver-domed **Mosque el-Aqsa**. The Dung Gate today provides access to the Temple Mount on which is located the third most important site for Islam, the **Dome of the Rock**—the site which Muslims believe is the place where Abraham nearly sacrificed Ishmael and which the Jews consider Abraham may have nearly sacrificed

---

4. Note the importance of three in tradition: e.g., three spikes said to be used in the crucifixion—two in the wrists and one in crossed legs.

Isaac—and the Mosque el-Aqsa. **Entrance to the Temple Mount** and both the Dome of the Rock and Silver Mosque is controlled and limited by the Muslim authorities, who are somewhat unpredictable.

The **Temple site** has had a significant history and has seen several important buildings erected on it. It lies directly to the north of the Ophel, or early city of David, and according to the Bible, **David purchased the site** from Araunah (Hebrew: Oman) the Jebusite to make an altar of thanksgiving to the Lord for halting the punishing plague after he took the census of the people (2 Sam 24:1–25 and 1 Chr 21:1–30), whereupon he vowed that the site would be where the Temple should be built (1 Chr 22:1). But instead of David being able to construct the **first Temple** (2 Sam. 7:6–16), **Solomon** built it in seven years (1 Kgs 6:37–38). It lasted some 360 years before it was destroyed in 587 B.C. by the Babylonians.

When the exiles initially returned, **Zerubbabel** began the construction of the **second Temple** about fifty years later, but because of frustrations with neighboring tribes, it was not completed for another twenty-two years. Little information concerning the structure

9. The author teaching his students at the model of Herod's Temple (now on display at the Israeli Museum)

is given in Ezra or elsewhere in the Bible, but it obviously was not as grand as the Solomonic Temple. In about 168 B.C. **Antiochus Epiphanes**, in response to Jewish resistance, performed the great **desecration** by having a pig sacrificed on the Altar of Burnt Offering and a statue of Zeus/Jupiter set up in the Most Holy Place (Dan 11:31–44). Three years later, Judas Maccabeus was able to recapture Jerusalem, cleanse the Temple, and as a result a new Jewish festival was birthed on the twenty-fifth of Kislev—the Feast of **Hanukkah,** or the Feast of Lights/Dedication.

Reconstruction and expansion of the Temple on a grand scale was initiated under the sponsorship of **Herod the Great,** probably the greatest builder of his time. A superb **model of the Temple and Jerusalem** (overleaf) during this period and before the destruction can be viewed in the complex of the Israeli Museum. Planning and reconstruction was begun in 20–19 B.C. and it was not finished until about A.D. 63, when it was destroyed by Titus and the Romans in A.D. 70.[5] This period is still referred to as the **Second Temple period** among the Jews because the Temple had not been destroyed but was merely reconstructed.

10. The magnificent Dome of the Rock on the Temple Mount

5. See John 2:20 for a reference to forty-six years for the building process in the time of Jesus.

The site lay in ruins for the years after its destruction until the period of the Bar Kokhbah Revolt under Simon ben Kosebah in A.D. 133–135. Emperor Hadrian then decided to end all Jewish access to Jerusalem and completely rebuilt the city as the Roman *Aelia Capitolina* with a Temple to Jupiter/Zeus on the Temple platform.

During the Byzantine period, the Christians concentrated not on rebuilding the site of the Temple but on building the Church of the Holy Sepulcher, which was believed to be the place of the crucifixion and resurrection of Jesus. Then during the Muslim period, Omayyad Caliph Abdul Ibn Marwan constructed the shrine known as the **Dome of the Rock** (*Harem esh-Sharifi*, 685–705; opposite). It certainly ranks as one of the most **beautiful** buildings in the world, and like all Muslim shrines or mosques those entering it must **remove their shoes**. The building contains **no pictures**, images, or other representations of humans, animals, or places but **only words** in conformity to the restrictions against making images and likenesses in Exodus 20:4 which are reaffirmed in Islamic teaching.

Nearby on the Temple Mount are the el-Fakhriyeh Minaret and the silver-domed Mosque el-Aqsa (which means "farther"). The entire site with the Dome of the Rock commemorates the translation of Muhammad from the "farther" Temple (Jerusalem) through the seven heavens into the very presence of Allah (see *Surah* xvii and xxxvii). The original Harem esh-Sharif was finished in 691 just about seventy-two years after the flight (*Hegirah*) of Muhammad from Mecca to Medina in 622, which is the starting point of the Islamic calendar.

The **Dung Gate** also provides access to the **Western Wall**, which is revered by Jews because of its nearness to the historic site for the Temple built by **Solomon**. The Western Wall has often been designated as the **Wailing Wall**, especially in the time before the Israelis controlled Jerusalem. But a better explanation for the connection to the idea of "wailing" is because in praying at the wall **Jews generally rock** back and forth, giving the impression of a sense of grief to those who do not understand their motions. The areas for approaching the wall assigned to men and women are **separated** by a fence and the **Torah scrolls** are kept in cases (arks) on the male side under the arches. **Men** frequently gather at the wall in **groups of at least ten** to pray and recite texts together.[6]

---

6. Contrast this with Paul's important thesis concerning no distinction/separation in Galatians 3:28.

11. *The Western Wall at the Temple Mount with separate courts for the men and women*

The Overlap of the Jewish and Armenian Quarters

The Final Gate is (8) **the Zion Gate**, through which the modern Israeli military conquered Jerusalem and which provides access to the **Armenian Quarter** at the upper level and the **Jewish Quarter**, which is slightly lower. In the Jewish Quarter, there has been a great deal of **archaeological excavation** conducted, and some of the Roman Streets (e.g., the **Cardo**) from the *Aelia Capitolina* have been uncovered, as well as earlier Jewish dwellings. Near the Zion Gate is the traditional site known as the *Coenaculum* (place of the Last Supper, **Upper Room**), which is obviously Crusader in construction but is a reminder of that strategic time in the life of Jesus and the early disciples (Mark 14:12–25). Below it is the traditional site of David's Tomb. These sites were undoubtedly developed during the Muslim period when movements were restricted for both Christians and Jews.

Nearby is the impressive domed **Dormition Abbey** of the Benedictine order. It was built over the site of an earlier Byzantine church called **Hagia Zion**, which was destroyed by the Persians. Later it was rebuilt and associated as a **traditional site for the death of Mary**. The church has an impressive gold-domed apse and a mosaic of the Virgin and Child.

Other Information Concerning Inside the Old City Walls

One of the sites that **intrigues visitors** to Jerusalem the most is walking though the crowded streets of the Old City where in the **bazaars** merchants sell their wares. Here one may find legitimate archaeological **lamps** and **coins** that have been certified by the Rockefeller Museum or fairly similar copies that may or may not be genuine antiquities. In the shops one can also find **carpets, jewelry**, pottery, ceramic wares, clothing, luggage, and many souvenirs, such as art work and **olive wood carvings** of various grades; however, care must be taken to obtain seasoned wood so that it does not split when one returns home to a heated house. Also in the shops there are available for purchase various spices, breads, and foods for eating including **pita sandwiches**. For those accustomed to finding meat in stores wrapped and neatly packaged, they will see **carcasses of lambs** hanging for sale in the market with the ends of their **furry tails** still attached so that the local purchasers can determine if the meat is fresh.

Another of the interesting places to be visited is the **Davidson Center** near the Temple steps, which in the time of Jesus led to the main Temple entrance. At this center one can watch a video presentation related to the Jewish Temple.

Outside and Around the Walled City of Jerusalem

We now move to the sites outside the walled city, traversing the area from the south to the west, then north, and finally to the east.

To the South Outside the Walled City

South of the Walled City and the Temple Mount is the small hill site called the **Ophel** (from the Hebrew meaning "swelling"), which was the old Jebusite hill city that was conquered by David and became the "City of David" (2 Sam 5:6–10).

Among the most interesting features open to visitors here is a portion of the **water tunnel built by Hezekiah** (ca. 702–701 B.C.) that brought water inside the lower wall to the Pool of Siloam from the Gihon Spring, thus creating Jerusalem as a siege city able withstand the attack of Sennacherib and the Assyrians (2 Chr 32:1–5). At the end of the tunnel an **inscription** was found in Hebrew (now removed to the Topkapi Palace in Istanbul) describing how the builders tunneling from both ends heard each other work and turned to meet, forming a reverse "s" shape in the tunnel.

Recently uncovered by **archaeologists** are the authentic ruins of the **Pool of Siloam** (south of the tunnel, displacing what earlier tradition assumed to be the pool over which was built a fifth century church destroyed by the Persians, now a mosque). From this pool the High Priest at the **Feast of Tabernacles** would carry a pan of water in holy procession to the Temple. After the hot summer, he prayed that God would return rains and water the land (cf. Jesus's words in John 7:37–38). To this **pool** Jesus "sent" (the meaning of "Siloam") the **man who was born blind** to wash the mud which Jesus made from his own spit and applied to the man's eyes in a new creation act that mirrored God's caring act of breathing into Adam the breath of life (cf. John 9:6–7 with Gen 2:7).

Further south from the Ophel and across the place where the valleys meet is another ridge that the Byzantine Christians (primarily **Jerome**) identified as the site of "**the evil council**," the traditional place outside of Jerusalem where **Judas** agreed to sell Jesus for **thirty pieces of silver**—the value of a slave for thirty coins—mirroring the earlier sale of Joseph by his brothers for twenty silver coins (Matt 26:14–16 and Luke 22:3–6; cf. Gen 37:25–28 and Exod 21:32). Later, Judas recognized his evil deed and tried to undo the act but was rejected, and after throwing the coins at the Jewish leaders, he committed **suicide** (Matt 27:1–5). The Jewish hierarchy reasoned that they could not put "blood money" in the Temple treasury for fear of annulling the Covenant (cf. Zech 11:12–14), so they bought a field for the burial of transients and called it a "**Field of Blood**" (Matt 27:6–10). Luke in an aside describes the demise of Judas more darkly by indicating that after the purchase of the field, Judas fell there and his body split open, causing his entrails to gush out (Acts 1:18–19). In both cases there was an attempt by the evangelists to explain the meaning of the site as a "Field of Blood" (*Akeldama*). Furthermore, between the City of David and this ridge that slopes into the Hinnom Valley is one of the places that early Christians identified as **Gehenna**!

West of the City of David and **south** of the Zion Gate on the southern spur of what has come to be known as Mount Zion is the Church of **St. Peter of Gallicantu** ("cock crow"), which was built in 1931 to commemorate Peter's threefold denial of Jesus (John 18:15–27). From this hill which overlooks the Kidron Valley and may have been the site of the High Priest's Palace, there are **steps** that lead down to the valley and could have been the route that the guards of the High Priest took **Jesus after arresting** him in the Garden of Gethsemane (John 18:12–13). In the lower basement of the church is a cistern, which could be the "temporary keep" for holding prisoners such as Jesus.

North and west of the church and overlooking the Hinnom Valley before it turns east is the site of the Institute for Holy Land Studies (**now the Jerusalem University College**), where the author taught for a brief period. In the cemetery of the Institute, the bodies of several nineteenth century archaeologists and people of note are buried. On the **southwest ridge** across the Hinnom Valley is (St.) **Andrew's Church of Scotland**, where the heart of Sir Walter Scott (the novelist who loved this land) is entombed.

To the West Outside the Walled City

At one time the **Hinnom Valley** marked the **border** between the tribes of Benjamin to the north and Judah to the south. Across the Hinnom Valley and on the **western ridge** overlooking Jerusalem is probably one of the sites where human children were offered to the **Ammonite god Moloch** (Jer 32:35 and Acts 7:43). Today on this hill is a unique **windmill**, which is a memorial to the modern Jewish patriot and founder of the New Jewish Jerusalem, Moses **Montefiore**. During the storming of Jerusalem in what the Jews call their War of Independence, the site served as the observation point for the Jewish fighters. Nearby is located a multi-chambered site that has been called the traditional **Herodian Family Tomb**. Herod, however, was buried on the Herodion near Bethlehem. North along the top of Hinnom ridge is the **YMCA** where traditional Jewish and Arab **folk dances** are performed for visitors to Israel.

To the North Outside the Walled City

North of the walled city and a few blocks from the Damascus Gate, as mentioned already, lies the **Garden Tomb**, the site which **General Gordon** identified as an alternative to the Church of the Holy Sepulcher. Here, most Protestant Christians on a pilgrimage to the lands of the Bible find a sense of spiritual refreshment because the place looks more like what they normally would expect to see in terms of a Skull Hill and a garden containing a tomb, with a channel used by a round stone in closing the burial site. Christian groups are offered the opportunity here to reflect on the death and resurrection of the Lord while conducting a worship service of the Lord's Supper (Holy Communion, or the Eucharist).

12. General Gordon's Garden Tomb north of the Old City

Also mentioned earlier, **north** of what is called Herod's Gate, is the famed **Rockefeller Museum**. Here many exhibits are on display, including the prehistoric skeleton of "Carmel Man" and reliefs from the palace of Sennacherib. Here, detailed work was done on the sorting and categorizing the many pieces of the **Dead Sea Scrolls** that were found in caves near the Dead Sea.

To the East Outside the Walled City and the Mount of Olives

East of the Walled City is the **Kidron Valley** (Valley of Jehoshaphat), which lies below the Mount of Olives and in which is located the **Gihon Spring** and **three large tombs**. These tombs are popularly designated as Absalom's Pillar (also called Jehoshaphat's tomb), Bnei Hezir family tombs (the grotto of James), and the Tomb of Zacharias, although any connection with biblical figures is doubtful.

I turn now to discuss the **Mount of Olives**. Most guides will take visitors to the top of the Mount of Olives and start down the hill because the climb uphill is quite demanding. At the **top** are several sites that traditionally mark the place where Luke indicates **Jesus ascended** from Bethany into heaven (Luke 24:50–51 and Acts 1:6–11). The **Russian Orthodox compound** is one of the high towers on the Mount of Olives that is also said by them to be the site of the **Ascension**. The place that claims the longest history is a small domed building covering the "Rock of Ascension," which is said to contain Jesus's footprint. The **Domed Chapel of the Ascension** was built here in the early Byzantine period, was partially destroyed by the Persians, and went through several reconstruction efforts, even during the time of the Crusaders. Some have suggested that it provided inspiration for the building of the Dome of the Rock on the Temple Mount. Nearby is the Greek chapel **Viri Galilaei**, which commemorates the instructions to the "Men of Galilee" (Acts 1:11).

*13. Overlooking the city of Jerusalem with Jewish tombs in the foreground and
Muslim tombs on the Temple Mount and the Kidron Valley between them*

North on this ridge is the site of the German **Augusta Victoria Hospital** that was named in honor of Kaiser Wilhelm's wife, and it contains a **tower** that overlooks Jerusalem and was built to remind people of the towers along the Rhine River. Further along the ridge is the Mt. Scopus campus of the **Hebrew University**, which was built at the close of the First World War and opened officially in 1925. During the time when the city of Jerusalem was divided and Jews were unable to cross the Green Line from 1948 to 1967, a new campus of the Hebrew University was built in West Jerusalem. Likewise, when the **Hadassah Hospital**, which was begun in 1939, was isolated, the Israelis built a new hospital on the west side of Jerusalem.

At the beginning of the descent from the Mount of Olives is a modern **Jewish cemetery**, where visitors will see a number of small stones placed on tombs. The **Jewish practice** is to place a **stone** on a tomb rather than flowers to honor the dead. Nearby is the

Pater Noster ("Our Father") Church compound where about four hundred large tiles containing the Lord's Prayer in various languages have been erected on walls to commemorate that portion of the Sermon on the Mount.

Midway down the Mount of Olives is the site where the Crusaders built a chapel to remember Jesus's weeping over Jerusalem (Luke 19:41–44) and which later was destroyed. The current beautiful chapel—called **Dominus Flevit** ("the Lord wept") and is in the form of a **teardrop**—now stands on the site, and it was designed by **Antonio Barluzzi**. In the same compound, visitors can see a tomb that contains a number of **ancient ossuaries** (burial bone boxes) in which people's bones would be stored in the burial chamber after the flesh decayed so that the **tomb** could be **reused** many times by the larger family. Those familiar with the **arguments** that have taken place between archaeologists over the **authenticity** of the **ossuary of James, the brother of Jesus**, will want to view this burial chamber. In the same area visitors will want to pause and view Jerusalem from this vantage point, then consider why Jesus wept over Jerusalem.

14. Ancient olive trees on the Mt. of Olives

Finally, north of the three large tombs in the Kidron Valley and situated near the base of the **Mount of Olives** are the Russian **Church of Mary Magdalene** (built by Czar Alexander III in the closing years of the nineteenth century); the **Garden of Gethsemane**, with its **ancient olive trees**; and the **Church of All Nations** (Basilica of the Agony) in which is contained the **stone** where pilgrims have traditionally said that **Jesus wrestled in prayer** before his arrest (Luke 22:39–46). This beautiful church with its twelve translucent small-domed alabaster windows reflecting various nations was designed and built in 1924 by **Antonio Barluzzi** and stands roughly on the site of an earlier (ca. 360–380) Byzantine church that was destroyed by the Persians. The **window for the United States of America** is immediately in the right-hand corner when entering the church.

Beyond the Immediate Vicinity of the Walled City

Today, Jerusalem stretches far beyond its earlier environs and continues to expand. New districts are being developed constantly. Indeed, major multilane roadways are gradually encompassing the old city, and the expansion efforts of new housing projects have created major tensions between the Jewish population and the Palestinians who sense that the Jewish city is fast closing in on them and their dream that Jerusalem would be the capital of a Palestinian state.

The Orthodox Section of Jerusalem

Both new and old sites are of interest to the visitor and pilgrim in the wider vicinity of Jerusalem. Among those sites the visitor will be interested in driving a little **north and west** of the old city through the **Mea Shearim** where the Jewish ultraorthodox **men** are dressed in black with their **black felt or fur hats and long beards** and the **boys** wear their embroidered **yarmulkes** (skull caps) and display their **curled locks** of hair. But care must be taken not to take motor vehicles into this section of Jerusalem near sunset on the eve of Sabbath because even buses can be stoned.

The Government Section and the Israeli Museum

West of the city is the **Knesset** (Israeli Parliament), surrounded by scores of buildings devoted to the various aspects of government. Visitors are naturally not allowed inside of the Parliament compound but may approach the entrance and **take pictures** of both the buildings and the large **menorah** (seven branched candle holder) that symbolizes the state of Israel. While the author was teaching Israel in the late '60s, he had the monthly privilege of visiting the Knesset for briefings along with other professors who were mostly Jewish.

Nearby is the **Israeli Museum**, which has multiple venues from the children's museum to the central archaeological museum with its vast store of treasures. Among the sites in the museum that visitors who have only a short time at their disposal find most enlightening are (1) the **Shrine of the Book** in which are displayed sections of the Dead Sea Scrolls and other allied finds, and (2) the **Model of Second Temple Jerusalem** (from the time of Jesus). This model was created under the direction of some of the foremost Israeli archaeologists and was first on display at the Holy Land Hotel. Today the site at the Israeli Museum provides multiple levels for viewing the earlier city.

Other Sites in New Jerusalem

Other sites worth seeing if the visitor has the time are: (1) the very modern **Hadassah Hospital**, which was built when the Palestinians prevented Jews from accessing the hospital on Mt. Scopus. In the synagogue at this hospital (just to the left of the main entrance) are located the **twelve magnificent stained glass windows** representing the twelve tribes of Israel, created by the well-known artist, **Marc Chagall**. Also worth a visit is (2) the **Kennedy Memorial**, composed of fifty-one struts with each over the seal of one of the states of the Union. The memorial gives the appearance of a great tree that was chopped off near the base of its trunk. Another site worth visiting is (3) **Mount Herzel**, where the heroes of Zionism and prime ministers and presidents of the Jewish state are buried.

Among the sites that all visitors to Jerusalem should visit, if they have the time, is (4) *Yad Vashem*, the **Israeli Holocaust Museum**, where visitors are given a full introduction to the Nazi pogrom (elimination effort) in which six million Jews were killed in Europe during the Second World War. Among the many displays and pictures in the museum that should make one pause are those such as the gold bar that was made from the fillings of the death camp victims' teeth, the memories of the Warsaw Ghetto, the touching children's memorial, and the solemn concluding memorial to the dead in the various camps. The trees that have been planted in the "**Avenue of the Righteous**" are a reminder of those who refused to acquiesce to the brutal actions of Hitler and his compatriots. In the library attached to the memorial are the files of many persons, and this writer had the opportunity to view some of them, such as the **Eichmann file**.

FROM JERUSALEM SOUTH TO BEER SHEBA

To Bethlehem

Leaving Jerusalem and driving south, one notices how much Jerusalem has grown over the past thirty or so years and now has extended beyond **Tantur**, where is located the international ecumenical study center that was once in the open countryside and is run by the Roman Catholics. There is very little open ground now between Jerusalem and Bethlehem. As one continues south, out of the left hand side of the car or bus one notes the more open spaces that face east towards the desert area, whereas on the right hand side there are still some substantial buildings evident.

On the eastern plateau **Herod the Great** built a **fortress** on the outskirts of the desert, which he called the **Herodion** (Herodium). Constructed on the top of a cone-shaped hill with a high, thick circular retaining wall and four towers, its exterior diameter was about 180 feet. The entrances were heavily fortified, and it was endowed with royal **amenities** including a **bathhouse** in the desert and a dining hall with a large *triclinium* ("U"-shaped table setting). The walls were finished in a fine stuccoed plaster that resembled marble, and it was enhanced with rows of **columns**. At his death, **Herod** was buried here, and his **tomb** was **discovered recently**. The fortress was occupied by **Jewish Zealots** who fought fiercely against immense Roman forces in both the Jewish war that saw the destruction of the Temple and the Bar Kokhba Revolt which ended in A.D. 135.

Closer to Bethlehem on the right side of the road is **Rachel's Tomb**, which for Jews is one of their most revered sites. The favorite wife of Jacob and the mother of Joseph (who received two allotments of land through his two sons), Rachel died giving birth to Benjamin **on the way to Ephrath** (Bethlehem; Gen 35:16–20). Today it is heavily guarded by Israeli soldiers. The text in Jeremiah 31:15 concerning **Rachel weeping** for her children has been interpreted by Jews to refer to their sufferings throughout the ages and by Christians following Matthew 2:17–18 as a fulfillment statement concerning the death of the infants under Herod the Great who sought to kill the infant Jesus. One interesting sidelight involves the tradition that when **Jewish women** are having difficulty conceiving, they frequently come to Rachel's tomb and **pray** that they might become pregnant.

Today, **Bethlehem** ("House of Bread") is inside the territory assigned to the **Palestinian Authority**. Visitors to Bethlehem must therefore carry their **passports** in crossing through the border. Visiting the traditional site of the **Church of the Nativity** is a special experience for pilgrims, for here is the site where **Queen Helena** after her research constructed the basilica to honor the birth of Jesus (one can still see part of the original floor). The church was later greatly expanded by Justinian and still stands today. Because of the mural of the wise men on the front of the church, it is the only church from the Byzantine period in Israel that did **not** suffer major **destruction** by the Persian forces as they swept through Palestine. The **front door of the church** is interesting because it reflects its history. The large door frame represents the Byzantine period when great doors could be opened. Then, after the early Muslim period, the Crusaders minimized the doorway into a smaller arched door for easy defense. Finally, during the later Muslim period, the Christians made a very small doorway, which necessitates crouching to enter so as to prevent enemies from riding their horses into the church.

Ownership of the church is **shared** by the Greek Orthodox Church (from 1672) and the Roman Catholic Church (from 1852). The earlier church has an ornate Orthodox iconostasis and many lamps and incense burners, whereas next door the Roman Catholic (Latin) Church of St. Catherine is much more simplistic. Below the main church in the cave (**Grotto of the Nativity**) is the large silver star that represents the traditional site where it is believed that Jesus was born. This star was placed there by the Roman Catholics in 1717 but was **stolen** by the Greeks in 1853, which resulted in a major conflict with the Turks who controlled the area, and it mushroomed into the **Crimean War**

15. The Grotto of the Nativity, the traditional site of the birth of Jesus

(1853–1856). Adjacent to the main cave is **another cave** in the Latin section, which is said to be the place where **Joseph in a dream** was instructed to take the baby and his mother and **flee to Egypt** (Matt 2:13). Nearby is also a **third cave** where **Jerome** is said to have spent his time translating the Bible into Latin (the **Vulgate**). Here Jerome died and was buried, but his body was later transferred to Rome and reburied in the Church of Mary Major. It is from this Roman Catholic Church in Bethlehem that the **Christmas Mass** is broadcasted around the world.

Eastward beyond the Church of the Nativity in the valley below are probably the locations of both the **fields of Boaz** where **Ruth**, the great grandmother of David, was gleaning (Ruth 2:1–16 and 4:21–22) and the **fields** where the **shepherds** were tending their flocks at night at the time they were **visited by the angel** who announced the birth of Jesus, and they heard the heavenly host proclaim glory to God and peace to humans who please the Lord (Luke 2:8–14).

To Hebron

Like Bethlehem, Hebron lies on the ancient road between Jerusalem and Beer Sheba. Today most visitors to Israel do not travel south to Hebron. But even prior to the establishment of the Palestinian Authority, few visitors traveled to Hebron unless they used a Palestinian taxi (sharoot) or bus because of the **volatility** of the situation there. Hebron had been known to be just a little different than other Palestinian sections of the country, and those who speak Arabic can tell you that the people of Hebron have a slightly **different dialect of Arabic** than those in the north. But the pattern for Hebron being a little different has been so for a very long period. Even in the time of **David**, that difference was one reason he made his **headquarters in Hebron** before making his capital Jerusalem (2 Sam 2:11). The remoteness of the south afforded him protection.

Hebron is an ancient city, probably founded as early as the eighteenth century B.C. (Num 13:22). Caleb conquered the city under Joshua and was allotted this area in the division of the land (Josh 15:13–14 and Judg 1:20). Hebron was also referred to as the so-called **Oaks** (*terebinths*) **of Mamre** and *Kiriath-arba* which could also refer to a "district" of Hebron (Gen 23:18 and 35:27). It was an early home for the nomad, Abraham, when he came to the land of Canaan, and at Hebron the Lord confirmed his covenant to Abram before his name was changed (Gen 13:14–18). Here, Abraham **buried** his wife **Sarah** after he purchased the field and the **cave of Machpelah** from Ephron the Hittite (23:1–20). Here, both Isaac and Ishmael buried their father Abraham (25:7–10), and here was also the place Esau and Jacob buried their father Isaac (35:27–28). For these reasons, Hebron has been significant to both **Jews and Muslims as a holy city**. Later, when Israel returned from Egypt, Hebron was designated as one of the cities of refuge where people suspected of crimes could flee in order to a have a fair trial rather than be dealt with by mob "justice" (Josh 20:7).

After the Exile, some of the returning Jews resettled there, but many of the inhabitants were Edomites who came to this region from the east side of the Dead Sea. As a result, the area from Hebron to Beer Sheba also became known as **Idumea**. **John Hyrcannus**, the victorious Hasmonean ruler who extended Jewish control over most of the territory that once was held by David and Solomon, conquered the lands of the Idumeans and forcibly had them circumcised. **Antipater and Herod the Great** were Idumeans! The city has been in continuous habitation; therefore, there has been little opportunity for archaeologists to do much in the way of excavation. Today, a great Muslim building complex surrounds the site of Abraham's cave.

To Beer Sheba

Pilgrims to Israel can readily visit Beer Sheba today, since it lies beyond the borders of the Palestinian Authority. Beer Sheba is the gateway to the **Negev**, or the southern desert. From Jerusalem one can either approach Beer Sheba by coming south along the Dead Sea and then turning west or traveling between the Palestinian territories of Hebron and the Gaza Strip.

The site of Beer Sheba is generally regarded as marking the **southern border** of the Land of **Israel**. Thus, the descriptions of Israel are frequently said to be from Dan (in the north) to Beer Sheba (Judg 20:1; 1 Sam 3:20; 2 Sam 3:10, 17:11, and 24:2, 15; 1 Kgs 4:25; 1 Chr 21:2; and 2 Chr 30:5).

The name **Beer Sheba** means "the **Well** (*beer*) of the **Oath**/Covenant (*shebuah*)" and is attributable to an event in the life of **Abraham** when the servants of King **Abimelech** of Gerar (located to the west of Beer Sheba) had a **dispute** with the servants of Abraham and seized the well that Abraham's people had dug. A **covenant of peace** between the two was subsequently concluded with seven lambs, and Abraham was therefore able to live in the land (Gen 21:21–34). Beer Sheba was like a **temporary home to the nomadic patriarchs**. From here, Abraham **traveled** to a mountain in **Moriah** and was successfully tested in his willingness to sacrifice Isaac. He was then able to return to Beer Sheba with the confirmation of God's blessing upon him (22:19). Isaac followed the pattern of his father Abraham in the dispute over the well at Beer Sheba and also concluded a covenant with Abimelech (26:17–33) but like his nomadic father, Abraham, ended his life in Mamre (Hebron) and was buried there (35:27–28). And it was at Beer Sheba that **Jacob** (Israel) made an offering to the Lord as he and his family were on their **way to Egypt** for his reunion with Joseph (46:1–5).

The prophet **Amos condemns Beer Sheba** along with Bethel, Dan, and Gilgal (Amos 5:5). It is not difficult to understand his condemnations of Bethel and Dan, because the golden calves were set up in each place by Jeroboam in his effort to redirect worship away from Jerusalem. And Gilgal, near Jericho, had benefitted from Samuel's frequent visits, even witnessing his slicing of King Agag to pieces (1 Sam 15:32–33). They had also known the works of Elijah and Elisha, so the judgments of Hosea and Amos were to be expected for their evil actions and false worship practices (Hos 4:14–15, 9:15, and 12:11; Amos 4:4). But why Beer Sheba? Recently, archaeologists uncovered the fact that alternative worship practices took place here as well, and their work included the discovery of an altar in this area. The people of Israel were plagued with temptations to syncretism. Is it any different today?

THE LOWER JORDAN AND THE DEAD SEA AREA

East of Jerusalem, the visitor will discover that the decent to Jericho is through a barren wilderness and is quite steep because Jerusalem lies in the mountains at about 2,500 feet above sea level; modern Jericho lies at about 800 feet below sea level; and the Dead Sea is now about 1,300 feet below sea level. Indeed, the bottom of the Dead Sea is another 1,200 feet deep.

The **wide modern road** that is cut through mountains and traverses the short **fifteen-mile distance** is hardly like the **ancient road** that was narrow with deep precipices and wound around the steep cliffs, making it easy to visualize the **story of the Good Samaritan** that Jesus told concerning the poor man who was attacked by thieves on the lonely road. So real could this visualization be that some entrepreneurs built an inn and identified it as the "Caravansary of the Good Samaritan." It has since closed, but visitors to the region should request their guide to leave the main road briefly and show them the treacherous valley that has been likened to the "valley of the shadow of death" in Psalm 23.

The Jordan Valley (also known as the Rift Valley) is the deepest cut in the earth's surface and part of the meeting of two tectonic plates that has created the great Pan-African fault that runs from the Sea of Galilee in the north through the Jordan Valley to the Dead Sea then to the Gulf of Eilat/Aqaba, is evidenced again in the Upper Nile River Valley, and runs to Lake Victoria in Central Africa. While the Gulf of Eilat/Aqaba and the Gulf of Suez appear on a map to look fairly similar, anyone who has been swimming off the **tip of the Sinai** at Ophira or Sharm-es (Sharm-el)-Sheikh knows that the Gulf of Eilat/Aqaba is exceedingly deep, and the other is relatively shallow by comparison. The one gulf has various types of bright colored fish and coral, the other does not.

The Area of Jericho

Jericho is one of the oldest inhabited sites (if not the oldest) in the ancient world, situated about six miles north of the Dead Sea. Its fortress (Tel el Sultan, which covers about ten acres and rises about sixty-five feet) served as a strategic city that blocked the important accesses to the central country of Israel and to Jerusalem itself. Also identified in the Old Testament as the "**City of Palms**" (Deut 34:3 and Judg 3:13), it is a beautiful oasis in a barren wilderness. It stood as a major impediment to the children of Israel in their goal of conquering their Promised Land. So **Joshua** dispatched two **spies** to provide him with information concerning the strength of its defenses before crossing the Jordan River (Josh 2:1–24).

Archaeology, the Tel and Ancient Jericho

The story of God causing the **walls** to collapse after the people encircled the city for seven days is known by most Sunday School students (Josh. 6:1–21). Therefore, first time visitors to the site are normally anxious to see the fallen walls. But besides viewing a **stone tower** at a lower level of the tel and noting the **burn line** in the strata, there is not much to be seen by visitors to Jericho.

I turn now to provide **a brief explanation concerning archaeological work** at the site for those who may be interested. Early archaeologists Warren (1868) and Garstang (1930–1936) made extensive excavations at the site. But it is from the composite work of Dame **Kathleen Kenyon's** evaluations (1952–1958) that some order has been achieved in our understanding of the tel, even though archaeology with Kenyon had not reached the sophistication of today.

16. The Neolithic stone tower in the tel at Jericho

The earliest remains at the site can be dated to between the tenth and the eighth millennium B.C., but since people were living in tents or small huts, not much was left to evaluate. During the excavation of the early Neolithic period a round tower (twenty-five feet wide) was found along with a portion of the wall. The size of the city is estimated to have been about 2,000 people at that time. About the sixth millennium B.C., the houses became larger and were made of brick. The stone pieces that were uncovered at the site were more advanced. Skulls were found embedded beneath the floors, suggesting some sort of worship pattern (perhaps of ancestors). By the fourth millennium B.C., the new inhabitants (presumably from beyond the region) buried the dead in hewn rock tombs. In the Early Bronze Age, there were multiple phases of building, while in the beginning of the Middle Bronze period the inhabitants (perhaps Amorites) did not seem to build substantial permanent structures and were likely nomadic shepherds. In the latter part of that period, small homes were constructed, and a wall built of mud bricks was found.

But these buildings easily crumbled in the long period that followed, when the site was apparently abandoned. In the later part of the Middle Bronze Age the city was rebuilt with homes in which grain and millstones were found, suggesting a fairly developed society. A substantial set of fortifications was also uncovered with a high supporting glacis (a constructed hilly foundation) surrounding the city, and a wall was built on the top. Bodies were buried along with food and drink and some accouterments, suggesting a connection with the Hyksos of Egypt. The city met a violent destruction (some suggest ca. 1550 B.C.) and lay in ruins for a long period in which the rains of the winter seasons would have washed away the remains of buildings. Little permanent habitation was found from later periods even though we know of some settlement after the ninth century B.C. and in the Late Iron Age, or Persia Period, but those remains have been washed away. Herod the Great built his winter palace elsewhere.[7]

The problem that remains is clarity on coordinating the dates of archaeology with the coming of Joshua in the Late Bronze Age. In addition, further confirmation of matters is difficult because the grid pattern for excavation was in its infancy and other disciplines of archeology were not yet developed. Moreover, because the method of disposing of the diggings was to remove the dirt to other places on the **tel**, the site has been virtually destroyed for further work. For those who had desired to see huge walls strewn around the site as though they imagined a castle from the Middle Ages might have fallen, it is imperative to remember that much of the city was made of **mud brick** and easily weathered, so not much has been left for viewing. Having taken many people to Israel for more than forty years, the author realizes that Jericho is often a disappointment to visitors. Yet, it is where an important aspect of Israel's history took place. The story of the fallen walls is important to remember because the eliminating of this major barrier to the Israelite advance was absolutely necessary, and it probably took much more than human ingenuity to prepare the motley crew of refugees from Egypt who had been camping in tents for forty years to conquer one of the great strongholds in the land of Canaan.

Jericho Today

Today the territory is in the hands of the **Palestinian Authority**, and unless visitors insist on seeing Jericho, it is usually not now placed on many itineraries because of the

---

7. See below, pp. 92ff.

time required for a visit. For those who do visit Jericho, in addition to the tel they can see an old **sycamore tree** like the one **Zaccheus** must have climbed (Luke 19:1–5). Many years ago, on my first trip to Israel, a guide tried to tell our group that it was the "original tree," but sycamores do not last that long. Fortunately, since that time, the guides are now certified, and they do not make such statements. The **Spring of Elisha**, which contains **fresh water**, is also located nearby (2 Kgs 2:19–22). The story points to the fact that in this area many of the springs coming from the hills do not usually give fresh water because of the minerals, particularly sulfur, through the deposits which the water flows. Accordingly, the **water** of most springs is **bitter** and has an odor, as the people of Jericho told Elisha. The fruit from Jericho is very sweet and makes great eating, but visitors are reminded to **peel or thoroughly wash all fruit** that is purchased in stalls before eating as they travel throughout the region.

Also, in this area are the remains of **Herodion Jericho**, containing the beautiful winter retreat of Herod the Great that had a great swimming pool where Herod had some of Mariamne's (a Hasmonean princess and his favorite wife) relatives (such as her brother, the high priest) drowned because Herod thought the family was trying to undermine his power. The site contains some fine mosaics and other amenities but it is basically restricted at this point to researchers and archaeologists.

The Dead Sea

The Old Testament writers usually refer to the **Dead Sea** as the **Salt Sea** (e.g., Gen 14:3; Num 34:12; Deut 3:17; Josh 12:3 and 15:2–5; etc.). It was also called the Sea of Arabah (Deut 3:17) and the Eastern **Sea** (Ezek 47:18 and Zech 14:8). It lies **1,292 feet below sea level** at the southern end of the Jordan rift between the Hills of Moab on the east and the barren Judaean Hills on the west. The name "Salt Sea" receives its designation because of its **high concentration of minerals**, which include mixtures of chlorine, potassium, natron, manganese, bromide, and calcium to mention only a few. As one might expect, the presence of these minerals has led to a vigorous **industry** at the southern part of the Dead Sea, which is quite shallow and allows for the establishment of large drying, or evaporation, pools. Among the valuable products that are harvested here are well-known **beauty creams** and **potash** for fertilizers.

17. Some of my students and others floating in the Dead Sea

The **salinity** runs between **thirty** and **thirty-three percent**, and, as a result, the Dead Sea has attracted **bathers** for centuries. It is not really a place for swimming because it is not advisable to put one's face in the water, but it is a great setting for floating or sitting in the water because it is virtually impossible for a person to sink in the Dead Sea. Many bathers enjoy covering themselves with mud from along the shore as a protective covering to prevent their skin from drying out if they intend to stay in the water for an extended period. Changing rooms and showers are available for minimal cost in a number of sites along the shoreline.

From what has been said above, it should be evident that the Dead Sea can be **divided into two segments:** the very **deep** northern section (ca. 1,200 feet) and the **shallow** southern section. Because so much water is being taken from the Jordan River system by Israel, Syria, and Jordan (an international river) for household and industrial use as well as for irrigation, the Dead Sea is shrinking in size, so visitors will easily recognize that establishments which at one time were on the shoreline and gave immediate access for bathing are now far inland and virtually abandoned. Some ancient records report that the Dead Sea used to reach the edge of the Judaean hills, so that in place of the open land where the modern highway has been constructed, it was necessary on the west side of the sea to take a boat to reach the southern extremities of the water.

Qumran and the Dead Sea Scrolls

Khirbit Qumran is located a short distance south of Jericho near the shore of the Dead Sea. It is probably the site of "**Salt City**," which is mentioned along with Engedi in Joshua 15:62. Even though the site was known for more than a century, it was not excavated until the **bedouins** found seven ancient scrolls hidden within a nearby **cave in 1947**. The find was probably the most electrifying manuscript discovery of the century because it produced **Hebrew biblical manuscripts** that were more than **1,000 years older** than any that were available before that time. Soon thereafter, the search began for more documents in the caves around Qumran.

Then from 1951 to 1956 in various campaigns, **Roland de Vaux** led a team of archaeologists in the **excavation of Qumran**. Today almost every pilgrim who has traveled to Israel has visited this site. Although scholars still debate the original use of the buildings, most are convinced that they belonged to a group of Essenes who lived as monks in the desert prior to and during the siege of Jerusalem under the Roman Imperial Commander Titus in A.D. 70. Father de Vaux, who himself is a monk and head of the well-established French School of Archaeology in Jerusalem, has been convinced that the site was a kind of monastery which housed **Essene monks** who practiced regular **lustrations** (full body baptismal washings) to ensure their purity and who engaged in the **copying of scrolls**. There is no question that the buildings at Qumran contain a number of water channels and pools that could be used for the purpose of such lustrations. Also, one of the large rooms where the top of a bench-like table was found, he designated as a scriptorium (a place where manuscripts were copied), and another large room measuring sixty-seven by thirty-five feet he identified as the assembly hall. His views have been widely accepted—even by the National Parks Authority—but some scholars have been doubtful of the connection between the building and the scrolls. An **alternative** suggestion is that

18. The author standing in front of the famous Cave 4 at Qumran

the building was a pottery factory, but this idea has not received general acceptance, although a potter's workshop with two kilns was found on the site and is said to have been a workshop for the community. Another hall is thought to have been used as a stable with troughs for animals. A large cemetery containing more than a thousand gravesites was also located to the east of the buildings. **Visitors** to the site are able to walk among the remains of the building and are able to view from the opposite hillside the site of Cave 4, one of the most important caves where some of the scrolls were found. They are now restricted from climbing on the hill itself both because weathering has made it dangerous and because of possible further damage to the site.

     One the scrolls that was discovered at Qumran is the *Manual of Discipline* (1QS, also sections of 4QS) which contains the rules and practices of the community. If such a scroll was related to the residents of the building, some have questioned whether they were Essenes or should simply be designated as the Qumran Covenanters. They were clearly against the priesthood in Jerusalem but it is still difficult to determine whether they were more like the Pharisees or the Sadducees. Such is the continuing saga of Qumran.

Among the scrolls that have been found are at least **portions** of **all** the books of the **Old Testament, except the book of Esther.** Several editions of **Isaiah**—one of which is in very good condition—were found, a copy of which can be seen in the **Shrine of Book,** a section of the Israeli Museum in Jerusalem.[8] Also included among the documents are early **commentaries** written from the perspectives of these covenanters, such as the Habakkuk Commentary (*Pesher Habakkuk,* 1QpHab) and other segments on Hosea, Micah, Nahum, a couple on the Psalms, interpretations of intertestamental works, as well as some **hymns** and early **Jewish liturgies.**

Engedi and Masada

South of Qumran between the Dead Sea and Judean Hills are located two historic sites, the one a beautiful oasis and hideaway associated with David and his flight from Saul; and the other a wilderness mountain fortress associated with Herod the Great and the Zealots who resisted the Romans.

Engedi (Ein-Gedi)

A **climb** to the **Upper Springs** of "Ein Gedi" (*ein* means "spring" or "fountain"), where the surroundings are green and pleasant, is a delightful experience in the wilderness for those who have the time and energy. The ancient name of the place was called *Hazazon-Tamar,* which means "pruning of the palm" because of the rich growth of palm trees in the oasis.

Here in hills and the strongholds of En-Gedi, **David** hid from the desperate Saul, who tried repeatedly to kill him (1 Sam 23:29 and 24:1). Here, **Jehoshaphat,** the King of Judah, and the people humbled themselves before the Lord and went forward to gain a great victory over the Ammonites and Moabites (2 Chr 20:1–30). Here, **Josephus** reports that in their resistance against the Romans and before the siege of Jerusalem, the **Sicarii**

---

8. Discussed earlier on p. 77.

("knife men," the fierce Jewish Zealots) after capturing Masada attacked and took the spoils of En-Gedi, but the Romans then reduced the town to rubble in A.D. 68 (*J. W.* 4.402). But after the destruction of Jerusalem, the **Romans** used the oasis as an important staging center for supplies and water in their battle against Masada. The Roman historian Pliny thereafter wrote concerning the site, "Lying below [south of] the Essenes was formerly the town of Engedi, second only to Jerusalem in fertility of its grove of palm trees, and now like Jerusalem a heap of ashes" (*Nat.* 5.73).

The Fortress of Masada

*19. The cable car at Masada with the remains of two Roman camps
that encircled the fortress in the background*

Masada is a high mountain plateau standing by itself out from the surrounding Judean Hills and rising more than 1,400 feet above the Dead Sea. It is located on the western shore, near the southern end of the deep section of the Dead Sea, about twelve miles south from En-Gedi. It was known as the mountain stronghold in the southern desert and according to **Josephus** (*J. W.* 7.285) was first fortified by the **high priest**, **Jonathan**, who was probably the brother and successor to Judas Maccabeus. Some have also suggested that it was Alexander Jannaeus (whose Hebrew name was also Jonathan). The site, however, was rebuilt by **Herod the Great** as his southern Judean link on the line of fortresses from Jerusalem to the Herodion to Masada to Machaerus on the other side of the Jordan Rift. In his early (40 B.C.) encounter with the Jews who hated his father, Antipater, Herod escaped to this stronghold with his family before making his way to Rome in order to be confirmed in his authority as Rome's voice in the area.

In rebuilding the fortress, Herod spared no expense in making it both **defensible and luxurious**. His main **palace** was built at the northern end's summit of the mountain on three levels descending from the top down. His personal quarters were on the lowest

20. Herod's hanging palace at Masada that descended from the top of the fortress

level and perched where few could reach him. The flat plateau above had an incredible system for **collecting the rainwater** on the top of the mountain and an additional means for accessing water from a reservoir in the nearby mountains if necessary. The amenities were palatial and the storage facilities so vast that it was unthinkable that he would run out of food or water.

The importance of these facts became clear in the time of the **Great Jewish Revolt** in A.D. 66, when a group of Jewish revolutionaries known as the Sicarii (radical "knife-men") took Masada from an unprepared small detachment of Romans who were stationed there holding the fortress. After the fall of Jerusalem, Masada became the focus of the Jewish resistance against the Romans. Therefore, in A.D. 73 **Flavius Silva**, the commander of the Tenth Roman Legion, was assigned the difficult task of taking Masada and capturing the resisters. With a force of 8,000 soldiers and auxiliary forces, as well as thousands of slaves and many prisoners of war, Silva encircled the mountain with a series of **eight camps**, which are still evident today. When he was repulsed in attempting to take the fortress via the narrow snake path and other minor means of entrance, he forced the Jewish slaves and prisoners to construct an enormous **siege ramp** of beaten earth and stones on the western side of the mountain. The Jewish freedom fighters refused to hurl stones or boiling water on their **captured Jews**, so the ramp continued to move forward. The Romans also constructed a **large siege tower and battering ram** and had it forced up the ramp. The Jewish resisters tried to burn the tower, but the flames blew the wrong way and caught their own defenses. So, the night before the Romans were destined to break through their defenses, the Jews on the mountain met in council. Flavius Josephus, the Jewish historian, reported what he considered to be the impassioned speech of **Eleazar Ben Yair** on that night as they faced the morrow. Among some of Yair's words were the following:

> Daybreak will end our resistance. But we are free to choose an honorable death with our loved ones. Let us leave this world unenslaved by our enemies, freemen in company with our wives and children. Let our wives die before they are abused and our children before they have tasted slavery. . . . But before we die, let us first destroy our money and let the whole fortress go up in flames: for I am well assured that it will be a bitter blow to the Romans to find our persons beyond their reach and nothing for them to loot. One thing only let us spare; let us spare our

store of food: it will bear witness that we perished not through hunger, but because we chose death rather than slavery according to our original resolution (*J. W.* 7.330–336).

Then, according to Josephus, the revolutionaries (a mere **960** men, women, and children) made a **suicide pact**. Each man killed his own wife and children. Then, each man lay beside his family to be killed by one of ten men selected by lot. After these men had killed the heads of the families, they cast lots among themselves and one of the ten was selected to kill the other nine, and finally he took his own life. The next morning, (2 May A.D. 73) when the Romans entered Masada, they found the smoldering ruins of the burnt houses and the eerie silence of death. Two women and several children hid themselves and were not partners in the mass suicide and thus were able to relate the story of those men, women, and children who chose death rather than slavery (see, *J. W.* 7.390–410).

After the Romans captured Masada, they maintained a military presence there until the second century. It then stood abandoned until a group of **Christian monks** took up residence there and built a small chapel at the center of the plateau. Despite the fact that **Yigael Yadin**, the director of the archaeological work done at Masada, thought he discovered the bones of the defenders of Masada, and the Israeli government ordered that the bones be buried with full military honors, it is at least a little doubtful that the bones were those of the zealots because Roman military practice was to bury bones of such people with those of pigs to defame them.

But Masada stands as an important memory in the conscious minds of Israelis, and many **recruits** have been inducted into military service on the top of Masada with the pledge that "Masada will not fall again."[9]

Accessing the heights of Masada is normally accomplished by riding the modern cable car nearly to the top, or for the stout of heart by climbing the winding snake path. Exiting the top can be done in those ways or by going down the Roman ramp, if one has arranged to be picked up on the opposite side of the mountain. Among the areas that should be visited on the plateau are the three-tiered northern palace, the three-room bathhouse, the room where the rebels chose their lots, the water gate, the synagogue, the breaching point of the Romans, the immersion pool, the western palace, the Byzantine church, and some of the cisterns. The views of the surrounding countryside from the top of Masada are spectacular!

---

9. For further information on Masada see the articles in the *Biblical Archaeology Review*, 24. 6 (1998), 30–54 and 64–68. See also Yigael Yadin, *Masada, Herod's Fortress and the Zealots' Last Stand* (London: Cardinal/Sphere, 1973).

A Note on Sodom and Gomorrah

The **"Cities of the Valley"** or Plain are described in Genesis (13:12 and 19:29) as the place which Lot chose when his herdsmen and those of Abraham came to dispute the feeding territory for their sheep. At least some of these cities were destroyed by **"brimstone and fire"** in God's judgment because of their wickedness (19:24). Among the cities in this group were: Sodom, Gomorrah, Admah, Zeboim, and Bela (14:3). The latter one was probably the smallest (since Zoar, the alternative name, means "little"), which is where Lot was hoping to hide (19:22).

While the remains of these cities have not yet been found, they were probably located on the eastern (Jordanian) side at the southern end of the Dead Sea (Josephus, *J. W.* 5.6–7) near the mouths of the four or five outlets for streams which flowed out of the southern Jordanian highlands. This valley was said to contain bitumen pits into which people could fall (Gen. 14:10). The ruins of these cities were likely submerged when the great Salt Sea rose. The area around the sea in this region has been known even in ancient times to have bitumen floating in the water (see, e.g., Tacitus, *Hist.* 5.6–7), and the Greek historian Strabo (16.2, 44), who spanned parts of the first centuries (B.C. and A.D.), also mentions that Sodom had been the major town among others in that vicinity.

Archaeologists found a significant fortress with thick walls of about fifteen feet in height along with a cemetery in the vicinity at *Bab edh-Dhra*, which is about 500 feet above the shoreline. This site, the abandonment of which can be determined from the pottery remains dated from around 2000 B.C., could have served several purposes: as a retreat in the cool hills during the intensely hot periods, as a gathering place for special celebrations or festivals, and as a place of refuge for people in time of war. It is fascinating that there is little evidence of permanent dwellings at this site, indicating that the people must have lived in the valley below. The concluding time frame for this site would coordinate with the period of the biblical story of the destruction of Sodom and Gomorrah.

ENTERING THE NEGEV

As indicated earlier, Beer Sheba is on the edge of the southern wilderness, or the Negev (which means "dry"). One also can enter the Negev south of Masada. A number of sites can be visited in this southern wilderness for those who have the time and inclination. Among those sites is **Tel Arad**, which lies about twenty miles east of Beer Sheba.

The **King of Arad**, who ruled the early Canaanite city, is mentioned in the Bible as **preventing the Israelites** from passing through his territory on the way to the Promised Land and indeed capturing some of them (Num 21:1). **Joshua** later defeated the forces of Arad in his conquest of the land (Josh 12:14). Then later the **Kenites**, descendants of Moses's father-in-law, joined forces with the people of Judah and moved from Jericho, the city of palms, to Arad and settled there.

The renowned archaeologists Yohan Ahironi excavated the **Israelite city**, while Ruth Amiran excavated the **Canaanite city**. Habitation began here as a small village in the fourth/third millennium B.C. (Early Bronze Age), growing into a prosperous center (ca. 2900–2700 B.C.) with a palace, shrines, and markets. It was surrounded by a fortified wall eight feet thick with semicircular towers. Even though it was in the wilderness, the inhabitants developed a **water collection** system by draining the rain from the streets into a large central reservoir that supplied plenty of water for normal city use and for irrigation, so the **city blossomed** and supported the breeding of sheep and cattle. But after a prosperous beginning, the site was apparently **abandoned** for 1,500 years (from the Late Bronze Age until a small Israelite city was built in the eleventh century B.C.). **Solomon** fortified the city in the last half of the tenth century B.C. and later kings expanded the fortress. Among the many ostraca (inscribed shards) found here is one that refers to "the **house of Jehovah** [YHWH]," which may be a reference to the Temple. The fortress continued to be occupied after the conquest of Nebuchadnezzar and into the beginning of the Roman period. It served as an inn during the Arab Period (seventh century A.D.) and was destroyed in the following century. It has not seen habitation since.

Nearby is situated the modern town of Arad, which offers hotel accommodations, and since it is nearly 3,300 feet higher than the Dead Sea, the cooling winds provide a respite for the visitor.

APPENDIX TO CHAPTER VI

The Issue of the Temple and the Temple Mount

One of the most intense political and religious issues in the Middle East concerns various debates with respect to the Temple Mount or what in Arabic is commonly called the Haram Al-Sharif in Jerusalem. One of those issues involves the fact that Israelis and Muslims differ in their traditions and proclamations concerning whether Abraham nearly sacrificed Isaac—or alternatively Ishmael—on a "Rock" which in this argument is said to be at the center of Temple Mount, a site which some would identify with Moriah (Gen 22:2). Another issue concerns the exact position of the temples of Solomon and Herod in relation to the "Dome of the Rock" and the Temple Mount itself. Indeed, debates have continued to swirl about since Dame Kathleen Kenyon's researches concerning the small size of the city of David on the Ophel and more recently as the result of Benjamin Mazar's work that questioned whether the Temple Mount was actually even the site for the ancient temple.

As I indicated in my introduction to Jerusalem, the city is regarded as an extremely sacred site to Jews, Muslims, and Christians, which means that religious and political concerns become an extremely significant factor in all historical and archaeological statements and investigations. It is even more so when it comes to the Temple Mount, or the Haram Al-Sharif. Indeed, the Israeli government does not usually interfere with the Muslim authorities on the Temple Mount, which is the third most sacred religious center in Islam and the designated site of the so-called midnight ride of Muhammad. Although the Israelis would like to do careful archaeological work within the Temple Mount, the Muslims are in charge, and they have been doing their own digging at the site and simply disposing of the materials in a haphazard manner. Some Israeli archaeologists, in response, have acquired those diggings and passed them through a screening and sifting process searching for any remains that might give some further clues to the unrecorded history of the site and assist in determining any implications which might follow. Moreover, the Israelis have charged that the Muslims in their digging under and near the al-Aqsa Mosque have been weakening the southern wall of the Haram and that the hasty repairs to the wall done by the Muslims are unsightly and completely inadequate to assure stability.

In contrast, excellent work done along the outer western wall has allowed visitors to walk along these foundations through a tunnel and see the huge foundation stones that supported the structure that formerly rose above it. But the big question that engenders disputes is: What was the structure above those great foundation stones, some of which stretch for 30 and more feet in length, are 15 feet in width, and stand over seven feet in height? Just to glimpse at the size of these gigantic stones is breathtaking. So the question that comes naturally is: Are not these huge stones part of the foundations for the temple?

In response, some scholars would remind us that no vestiges of earlier temples have been found on the site with the exception of representations of Mars, the Roman god of war. Yet such a situation might not be unexpected given the harsh decrees of Hadrian. The discovery of artifacts praising the Roman generals like Hadrian and those from the time of the fall of Jerusalem in A.D. 70 like Titus and his understudy Silva who captured Masada, however, give us cause to take care about drawing hasty conclusions concerning Jewish worship at this site.

We know that Herod the Great built the Antonio Fortress north of the temple. We also know that the temple was destroyed in A.D. 70 and that after the Bar Kokhbah revolt Hadrian decreed that in punishment for the rebellion all vestiges of Jewish Jerusalem should be obliterated. The city was rebuilt according to a typical Roman plan with a great Cardo and the city was called Aelia Capitolina. Furthermore, all Jews were excluded from the city on pain of death. Remains of that Cardo have been uncovered by archaeologists and so also have the walls from the earlier time of Hezekiah. To enhance the punishment, the territory south of the Haram (the Ophel) was designated by the Romans as a place for the disposing of trash.

We also know that the Christians in the Roman period had little interest in the Haram (Temple Mount) since their sacred site was further west at the Church of the Holy Sepulchre, which Queen Helena later officially designated as the place commemorating the crucifixion and resurrection of Jesus. In the post-Roman period the Haram stood abandoned and in the Muslim period it was appropriated for a mosque which has since become a very significant religious site.

Many years have now passed and part of the Antonio Fortress was thought to have been uncovered in the basement of the Sisters of Zion Convent just north of the present day Temple Mount. If this conclusion still has validity, the question remains concerning how large in fact was the Fortress of Antonio? Flavius Josephus seems to indicate that the Romans may have quartered a legion of between five and six thousand military personnel in the fortress so it is questionable whether the small area around the convent would have been adequate to house such a force. One must, therefore, ask the further question: Did the fortress extend onto the Temple Mount? Such a theory would seem to be rather plausible. The accompanying question then is: Did those Herodian stones serve only as the foundation for the fortress or for both the temple and the fortress? That question certainly has been the focus of debates among some scholars.

A number of archaeologists today believe that the temples of Israel and Herod were actually built south of the Haram (Temple Mount) and that the walls and the platform served only as the site for the Fortress. Now it is beyond dispute that Herod built the fortress in order that it would overlook the temple so that its proceedings could clearly be observed. Indeed, when Paul/Saul was being mobbed and dragged out of the temple, the Roman tribune was on the scene very quickly (Acts 21:31). Was the temple then constructed on the Haram or on the upper Ophel below the Temple Mount? Unfortunately the Arab houses that currently occupy the site do not at present permit thorough archeological investigation but some work is nevertheless still proceeding under those buildings. Yet, it may be that this area will never be fully examined not only because of Arab ownership but also because of the ramifications of such research. It is possible that even some Israelis may not really want to know the answers, although such suggestions have actually been posited by scholars for years. The Western Wall (frequently called the Wailing Wall) is now very ingrained into the Jewish mindset, so the question arises: What would it mean for Jews to be worshiping next to a hated Roman military center when since the Middle Ages they had thought it was a place that goes back to David and Solomon? The idea of subjecting the upper Ophel to major archaeological research could be a political nightmare. Kenyon had earlier suggested that the city of David was not as big as was sometimes thought. So, if the temple would have been below the Haram (Temple Mount), lying lower and nearer to the Gihon Springs than was generally thought, then a number of implications would naturally follow and many theories would have to be revised. This suggested placement of the temple would certainly fit with the historical reports that the temple had an abundant supply of fresh, running water in comparison to the supply on the Haram (Temple Mount) where the water is collected in the more than 30 large cisterns like those visitors can see at the Sisters of Zion.

On the other hand, the arguments are not only on one side because even though one could admit with Kenyon that the city of David was smaller than earlier imagined, the question still might be asked by some: Would it be possible that little if anything has survived from the huge platform that would point to the magnificent temple that was initiated under the supervision of Herod, the greatest builder of his time, who dreamed great fortresses like Masada and the Herodian and magnificent memorials to his ingenuity such as Caesarea Maritima and his summer palace at Jericho? Is only the Antonio Fortress left to recall the vast temple complex described by Josephus and alluded to in Mark 13:1? If so, the prediction of Jesus in verse 2 would certainly be fulfilled far beyond anything anticipated. But one must still explain the great cornerstone that crashed down from above and shattered the walkway below the present-day corner of the southern and western walls of the Temple Mount (Haram). This large stone seems to give some evidence that it was the so-called trumpet "pinnacle" of the temple, the point from which the call to worship could sound forth. The presence of this stone needs to be explained. So the questions continue.

But in concluding this brief APPENDIX, it is probably imperative for the writer at this point to help refocus the thinking of those Christians who in their eschatological zeal sometimes have considered that the "Dome of the Rock" would need to be destroyed in order that the Jewish temple could be rebuilt so that Jesus could return in power. While such thinking not only reflects a poor understanding of eschatology, it also evidences a truncated view of God's power as being subject to human initiative and it lacks a genuine sense of respect for the religious perspectives of other people, such as the Muslims. But more to the point, one could also add that if, as a number of scholars are now suggesting, the temples of Israel were not even built on the Haram (Temple Mount), then the whole question of rebuilding the temple on the Temple Mount is moot anyway.

VII

MATTERS RELATED TO TRAVEL IN ISRAEL

TABLE 7.1

APPROXIMATE DISTANCES IN ISRAEL

Dan to Beer Sheba (**as the crow flies**)	146 miles

OTHER DISTANCES

Jerusalem to Alexandria (Egypt)	320 miles
Jerusalem to Bethlehem	7.5 miles
Jerusalem to Caesarea Maritima	72 miles
Jerusalem to Capernaum	105 miles
Jerusalem to Damascus (Syria)	185 miles
Jerusalem to Jericho	15 miles
Jerusalem to Masada	67 miles
Jerusalem to Nazareth	101 miles
Jerusalem to Samaria	36 miles
Jerusalem to Tel Aviv	42.5 miles

Currency

The Shekel is the basic medium of money in Israel with 100 agorot to one shekel. But visitors to Israel do not need to change dollars into shekels. Merchants in Israel, Jordan, and Egypt readily accept dollars in payment for merchandise. In fact many prefer it to local currencies.

Guides: Israel and Palestinian Territories

The guides in Israel proper are among the best in the world and are clearly comparable to the guides in Greece who have been regarded for years as superb. The guides in Israel today are required to be conversant in matters of archaeology, history, and the Bible. Whether they are Palestinian Christians or Israelis, visitors on pilgrimage to Israel will find them very knowledgeable, not only concerning the Old Testament but also the New Testament. Tested rigorously in order to become certified, they are a far cry from my first guide whom I mentioned earlier relative to Jericho, or my first guide in Ephesus whom I had privately to inform that I had written an encyclopedia article on Ephesus and would be happy to help him if necessary. You should not encounter mere folk traditions about sites from the guides in Israel.

When a change of guides is necessary as you pass into the Palestinian Territories, the situation is not quite as positive, but Christian guides are trying to learn their tasks and are generally making good progress in their efforts. Visitors should be sensitive to their learning curve and not be too demanding.

SECURITY MATTERS

One of the **burning questions** that I am asked by persons contemplating traveling to Israel and other places in the area of the Fertile Crescent concerns security. I have been in most of the Fertile Crescent and on **both sides** of the conflicts in times of tension and even during periods such as the so-called Six Day War. During these times I have **not felt unsafe** because I try to follow the acknowledged guidelines for being in those countries.

If one is **traveling in a group with a certified national guide**, one should understand that the guide will be in **contact with security forces** and will not take you to places that are regarded as unsafe. **Tourism is a major industry** in that part of the world and each country understands tourists must be guarded in order to safeguard the revenues of that country and other neighboring countries as well. **Cellular phones** have made the task of communication in terms of security far easier than it was in previous years, and one can be certain that guides and security forces use them. Remember that what happens in one part of the Middle East affects all the other parts.

All travelers when journeying in foreign lands should observe **common courtesy**. When **traveling with a group**, try to consider that the group patterns are not the primary guidelines for that area because **customs are different** from place to place and visitors should seek to learn the customs of each place, such as remembering that **kosher** restaurants will not serve milk with meat unless they have a milk substitute; so, if someone wants coffee with a meal (one usually expects to have cream or milk served with the beverage), one might have to wait until after the meal and have coffee at the coffee bar. If one is **traveling as an individual**, it is even more essential to observe the customs of the area. Please do not make yourself an example of the **ugly, demanding American**, whom I have encountered in various places around the world.

But beyond these general comments, let me add some other bits of advice:

TABLE 7.2

— **Guard your passports** and keep them in a secure place unless the travel company requires them.

— **Neck pouches** can conveniently be used, especially by men for passports and money or traveler's checks.

— **Traveler's checks** may be cashed at banks and major hotels but a service fee is usually charged.

— **Major shops accept credit cards**, but check with your guide or tour director to make sure that the shop is known to be reliable. Remember that most credit card companies are now charging fees for **exchanging** foreign currencies into dollars.

— **Warning concerning PICKPOCKET TEAMS**: There are certain places in Israel and elsewhere where pickpockets are at work. Particularly in Jerusalem at crowded places, such as on the hill coming down from the top of the Mt. of Olives to Gethsemane and in the Old City one should watch out for them. I have had a few people lose either a camera or a wallet in theses places. Thieves are sly, fast and work in teams. To be **forewarned** should be sufficient to be safeguarded.

VIII

VISITING THE SINAI AND THE WILDERNESSES

CROSSING INTO THE NEGEV and the Sinai is an important experience for the visitor to the lands of the Bible. Few people who are familiar with the stories of the Exodus can fail to sense that it takes a hardened people to live in the Negev or the various wildernesses (of Shur, Paran, Etham, and, of course, Sin in the south). As I indicated in the Preface, my first visit to the Sinai was just after the Israelis had captured the Sinai from Egypt, and there were no hotels there except in Eilat on the edge of the Sinai (or Aqaba on the edge of the Arabian Peninsula), sites that would have been near the biblical **Ezion-geber** (Num 33:35–36), where Solomon had his southern fleet on the shores of the Gulf of Eilat/Aqaba (1 Kgs 9:26 and 2 Chr 8:17).

THE SINAI WILDERNESS

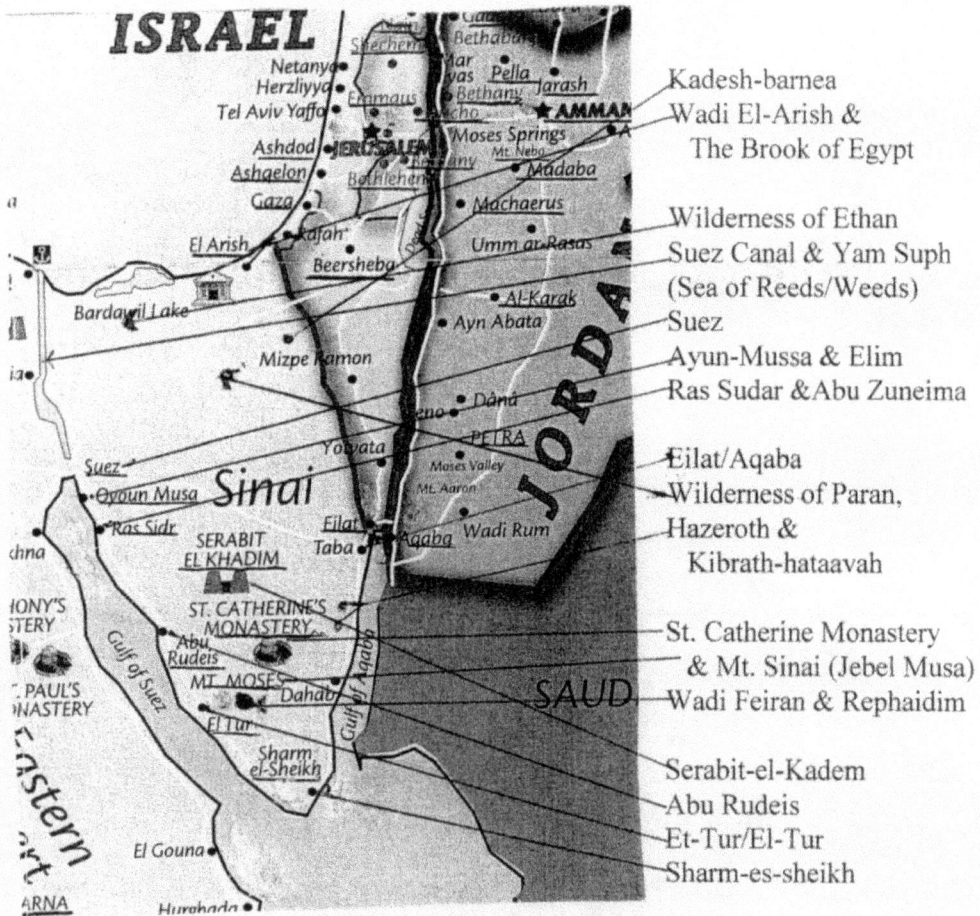

Our expedition of biblical professors from America that journeyed in two large six-wheel drive army vehicles, traveled where there were few if any roads then, slept in bed rolls, ate food cooked over outdoor fires, and discussed the Exodus around those campfires. These experiences seared into my memory the travels of the people of Israel as they wandered in the wilderness for many years. The Sinai has been both rugged in its beauty and before the present day harsh for those who were not prepared for wilderness living. Unlike the Israelites who depended on God for their supplies, we carried our food and water in the trucks. And in this venture, we carried our large water bottles as we climbed the various mountains, wandered over a number of long abandoned Tels and found small flint items from a long-ago era, felt the winds of the desert on our cheeks, and experienced the chill that comes over the sandy dunes when the sun goes down. But the Sinai is not all sand. We had an exciting time visiting some unforgettable sites such as the mountain hideaway where the Egyptians mined their turquoise and left their accounts on stone markers (stelae/steles) in what otherwise might look like a cemetery with standing stones—Tuvia's Forest, where volcanic ash covered reeds and then hardened so that they

21. *The author near one of the stone reeds of Tuvia's Forest in the Sinai*

became strange rocky spikes with hollow cores, and the peculiar encounter on the shore of the Gulf of Suez with plants that drank salt water and then shed the salt through their leaves. Those were experiences that provided this traveler with insights into a world that most of us normally do not encounter. What I am saying here is: Be prepared to have an interesting time in the Sinai even if you stay in a modern hotel during your visit.

Even though there was nothing much at Sham-el Sheik (the tip of the Sinai) on my first trip to the Sinai, if you stay for a day or so you can still snorkel off that tip today while staying in a modern hotel. You can learn the amazing fact that while the Sinai looks on a map to be a **V-shaped chunk of land** surrounded by two bodies of water called gulfs, those gulfs are radically different. The **Gulf of Suez** on the west is a normal body of water but the **Gulf of Eilat/Aqaba** is part of the Pan-African fault which is one of the deepest cuts in the earth's surface and which contains **coral** and **brightly colored fish** just like the coral reef north of Australia.

North in the Sinai

If your **visit to the Sinai is only a brief** travel along the coastal highway (the route near the old Via Maris) that leads now directly to crossing the modern Suez Canal, you will be passing through the vast region which is known as the **Wilderness of Shur** and joins Israel's Negev. Here Hagar found a spring in the desert (Gen 16:9), and south of here near Gerar is where Abimelech mistakenly seized Sarah, the wife of Abraham (Gen 20:1–3), to make her part of his harem. Into the **western part** of this wilderness the people of Israel entered as they left the **drowned Egyptian army** en route to the Promised Land. But as they began their southward trek to Mount Sinai they soon encountered the bitter waters of **Marah** that were made sweet when Moses called for the help of the Lord (Exod 14:27–15:25).

Just over fifty miles (eighty-two kilometers) south of Gaza and about 125 miles (200 kilometers) east of Kantara and the Suez Canal along the modern highway lies the **Wadi El-Arish**, which has often been identified as the **Brook of Egypt**. The southern extremity or border of Israel has sometimes been described in terms of this "River" or the "Brook" of Egypt (Num 34:5; Josh 15:4 and 47; 1 Kgs 8:65; 2 Chr 7:8; and Isa 27:12). Scholars are hesitant to suggest that this reference to the river or brook refers to the Nile River, so the alternative has been to suggest that the generally dry river bed (wadi) located in the midst of the Sinai may be the meaning intended by the biblical writers.

For those who will **spend a longer time in the Sinai**, they will find that on the **eastern edge** of the Wilderness of Shur, the southern edge of the Negev, and north of Eilat there lies the important **oasis of Kadesh-barnea** which is about **fifty miles south of Beer Sheba**. Here, after journeying mostly in the southern Sinai for about two years, the Israelites set up camp. Then in preparation for entering and capturing the land of Palestine/Israel from the Canaanites and other tribes, they **sent out twelve spies** to determine the strength of the Canaanites who lived there. All except two, however, came back with a **discouraging report** concerning the strength of the enemy, which led to Israel's further desert experience for another thirty-eight years (Num 32:8 and Deut 2:14; cf. Num 13:1–33). **Some scholars** believe that the people of Israel might actually have stayed in the region of Kadesh-barnea (or Meribath-kadesh) for up to thirty years more, during which time many of the **elders died.** If this suggestion is correct, then the places where Aaron died on **Mt. Hor**[1] may have been in this region and Meribath. Where **Moses struck the rock** in disgust because of the rebellious people would also be in this area (Num 20:1–13 and Deut 32:48–52). The basic **problem** is that those texts refer to the place as the "Wilderness of Zin" which may be another name for this wilderness, or the writers may have simply expanded the territory normally designated as the southern Wilderness of Sin to include all of the Sinai.

South in the Sinai

We now turn to the southern segment of the Sinai, which is by far the most interesting,

Eilat and the Southern Border of Israel

Modern borders are established for political reasons. The current V-shaped narrow neck of land that forms the most southern part of Israel is a small section of the **Wilderness of Paran** providing Israel with access to the **Gulf of Eilat/Aqaba** and thus to the Indian Ocean. The **city of Eilat** has become Israel's principal winter **resort** and a year around place for rest and recuperation. Statistics reveal that it rains here only about once

---

1. See below concerning Horeb.

a month from November to March and virtually never in the other seven months of the year. Since the gulf here is part of the great Rift Valley and the Pan-African Fault, anyone who spends a little time in Eilat should take a short trip on a **glass bottom boat** from Eilat in order to view the brightly colored marine life that inhabit the gulf.

Near Eilat at **Ezion-geber, Solomon** established his **southern port** for bringing prized imports from southern Arabia, Africa, and the Orient. The port was his special harbor for importing the gold from Ophir in southern Arabia, which probably came originally from Africa (1 Kgs 9:28 and 2 Chr 8:17–18). This **trade in gold** was exceedingly significant and **continued long** after the division of the kingdom, since the Bible mentions that Jehoshaphat's gold bearing ships were destroyed at Ezion-geber (1 Kgs 22:47).[2]

To Jebel Musa (Mt. Sinai) and the Monastery of St. Catherine

Traveling south from Eilat in reverse order to the itinerary of the ancient Israelites, the visitor will see a variety of panoramas in the **Wilderness of Paran**, and they should pass **Hazeroth** where **Miriam** was inflicted with leprosy after she and Aaron tried to supplant Moses by condemning him for marrying a Cushite woman (Num 12:1–16). Then we continue south on the eastern edge of the Sinai to **Kibrath-hataavah**, where the Israelites complained bitterly that they had no meat, and thereafter the Lord sent quail causing many of the people to die when they stuffed themselves with the food (Num 11:1–35). Finally, one arrives at the area that draws many visitors and pilgrims, the site identified as **Mt. Sinai**.

Climbing Jebel Musa (the **Mountain of Moses**) can be a thrilling experience—especially if one is into mountain hikes—but the climber should **start the ascent several hours before dawn** in order to experience the rising of the sun on the mountain (we started at 2:00 A.M.). The mountain rises to 7,362 feet above sea level and 2,349 feet above the valley where the large monastery is located.

The climb is not difficult until after one passes the **memorial** set up to remember the **pouting Elijah's** encounter on **Mt. Horeb** with the "**voice of silence**" (as the Hebrew indicates, not "still small voice"), after it became clear that God was not in the great wind, the earthquake, or the fire (1 Kgs 19:9–18). The rest of the climb, though more strenuous, has been made easier by the steps that have been carved in the mountain making the

---

2. For a perspective on the significance of this trade, note the harsh condemnation of Babylon in Isaiah 13:12 where those who are left after God's judgment will be more rare than the gold of Ophir.

climb for pilgrims more manageable. **Most visitors**, however, remain below **in the valley** and imagine what it must have been like for Moses to ascend into the cloud, **encounter the holy God,** and receive the historic **Ten Words/Commandments.**

The designations **Mt. Horeb** and **Mt. Hor** are a little unusual. While Mt. Hor has been identified in the past with Jebel Harun in central Edom, on the top of which is a mosque honoring Aaron as the high priest, perhaps it is better to recognize that "Hor" like "Har" in "Har Megiddo" simply means "mountain" or a significant hill. By this point in one's pilgrimage it should be evident that there has been a tendency on the part of pilgrims to combine **places of pilgrimage**. As a result, the two important mountain experiences for the heroic figures of **Moses** and **Elijah** have often been linked together, and thus **Sinai** and **Horeb** have been synthesized for the convenience of the faithful. If you ask the question, "Are we even sure that Jebel Musa is Mount Sinai?" the best answer is that Jebel Musa is the traditional site assigned to the experience by people in the past. Certainty concerning the place, however, is not possible.

22. The bell tower at the Monastery of St. Catherine in the Sinai

Clearly the founding of the **Monastery of St. Catherine** at the foot of Jebel Musa attests to an early tradition concerning this site. The monastery, one of the oldest in the world (sixth century), was built at the instruction of Emperor Justinian and is dedicated to a famous fourth century Egyptian female martyr whose bones allegedly were carried by angels to this mountain. It is said that the church in the monastery is built over the place **on Mt. Horeb** where Moses encountered **the burning bush** that was not destroyed and where God called him to service (Exod 3:1–6). As one might anticipate, a beautiful mosaic under the apse of the church is dedicated to the **Transfiguration** wherein Moses and Elijah are seen with Jesus. Visitors may also be given the opportunity to see the small room which is the holiest part of the monastery and which is said to be the actual spot where the burning bush was located. One is allowed to enter here on the condition that one agrees to accept all **responsibility of a curse** for approaching the holy place **wearing shoes.**

One of the interesting parts of such a visit here is seeing the **collection of bones** that are typical in many of the early monasteries throughout the Mediterranean world. The **bones** of the residents after death and the decay of the flesh are **separated** and placed together with the bones of former members of the order. Thus, the **skulls** are collected together as a symbol of their union in the holy fellowship. In visiting sites such as this one, it is important for today's pilgrims to understand that ancient pilgrims linked **memories to places** for the purpose of honoring not the places but the memories. As one visits a monastery like St. Catherine and sees the **icons** and other items that are revered, please remember what those items mean to the residents of the fortress, which is home now to only a few monks that are still there.

I must not conclude this brief discussion of this monastery without mentioning the visit of Count Constantine von **Tischendorf** who discovered one of the earliest manuscripts of the Greek Bible here. He claimed to have found the monks using it for kindling and rescued it by taking it to the Russian Czar, who in turn knighted him for his find. This priceless manuscript—now called **Codex Sinaiticus** (א, Aleph)—was later sold by the Russian Communists for £100,000 sterling to Great Britain, where it is housed in the British Museum. The monks, however, will show you a letter indicating that Tischendorf agreed to return the manuscript to their library once he had studied it and shown it to the Czar and other scholars.

To the Wadi Feiran and the Great Oasis

If one assumes that Moses led a large band of Israelites out of Egypt and into the southern Sinai, the next question that naturally is posed concerns where would they camp and have the necessary water in the Wilderness of Sin. The most likely place would be the area of the Wadi Feiran.

23. Palm trees in the oasis at Wadi Feiran

But this area that encompassed the great oasis was also frequented by the fierce camel-riding, **nomadic Amalekites** from the north who viewed the Sinai as their domain and attacked caravans and travelers at will, pillaging villages and destroying anything in their way. Here in this area, these fierce nomadic fighters at Rephidim attacked the Israelites. **Joshua**, who **comes to our attention** at this point as a warrior leader, mobilized the Israelite fighters against these nomadic raiders and won the battle while Aaron and

Hur ascended the nearby hill and held up the hands of Moses as a sign that the Lord was fighting for the Israelites (Exod 17:8–16). Guides along the way will probably point out a place where **tradition** suggests that **Moses sat and lifted his hands** while Joshua was engaged in the battle.

Prior to the battle, there is a story of Moses **striking the rock at Massa and Meribah** near Rephidim to supply the Israelites with water and in so doing **testified to the presence of the Lord** in their midst (Exod 17:1–7). There is also a strange mirroring of this story in the latter account in Numbers 20:1–13 (mentioned above) where Moses struck the rock **in anger** at Meribah near Kadesh-barnea, and God condemned him for failing to honor him.

After the Israelites had traveled south from Egypt along the Gulf of Suez through the parched desert of the Wilderness of Etham and complained numerous times to Moses, their **arrival at the Wadi Feiran** with its **beautiful palm trees and water** supply must have appeared to them to be like a new Garden of Eden. For the traveler today, the great oasis is still a very welcomed sight in the midst of the wilderness.

To the Southern tip of the Sinai

For those who are able to travel to the Southern tip of the Sinai as I have noted above, the experience is **delightful**. The town of **Sharm-es-sheikh** (sometimes called Ophira) is located on a small bay by the same name ("Bay of [an unnamed] Sheikh") or as the Israelis refer to it, Mifrats Shelomo ("Bay of Solomon"), near the narrow entrance to the Gulf of Aqaba/Eilat. Some have speculated that the name **Ophir** originally was a territory in Africa from which the name "**Africa**" was derived. Nearby in a **resort area** that the Israelis named Na'ama ("lovely" or "pleasant"), after Solomon's wife and mother of Rehoboam, are a number of fine hotels that host many conferences. **Scuba diving** is a perennial sport here.

To the Eastern (Gulf of Suez) Side of the Sinai

In terms of the contemporary world, **Abu Rudeis**, located about 125 miles north of Sharm-es-sheikh, is perhaps the most **important city** in the Sinai. In this vicinity, visitors will find the **oil fields** of the Sinai. Midway up the coast to Abu Rudeis is the important town of **et-Tur** (Arabic for "the Mount"), which has been the main **quarantine station for pilgrims** from Egypt en route to the **holy Muslim cities in Arabia**.

About twenty miles north and in the surrounding mountains near Abu Zuneima and Ras Sudar, **manganese** is quarried for Egypt today. In ancient times on the top of **Serabit-el-Kadem** ("the Monument of the Servant [of God]"), the visitor to the Sinai will find the temple dedicated to the **Egyptian cow goddess**, **Hathor**, who was the **guardian of turquoise**, the prized stone that the Egyptians used in the making of their jewelry. The Egyptian nobility sought to keep the famous cave (el-Meghara) where the mining took place hidden from outsiders, but the area around the cave has many hieroglyphic monuments describing the campaigns of the Egyptians into the wilderness in their goal of gaining the semi-precious stones.

24. Meeting bedouins at a northern oasis in the Sinai

A few miles north of Ras Sudar and after crossing several wadis, the Sinai visitor soon comes to another **major oasis** that is named **Ayun-Mussa** (the "spring of Moses"), which undoubtedly was visited on the journey of the Israelites as they traveled south to Mt. Sinai. The text of Exodus 15:27 indicates that there were seventy palm trees and twelve springs at **Elim**. These numbers "**seventy**" and "**twelve**" are frequently used in the Bible to indicate significant events or phenomena in terms of their "completeness" or adequacy. Actually here at Ayun-Musa there are hundreds of palm trees in the oasis and sufficient water for a large group of people.

Proceeding north into the Wilderness of Ethan the territory becomes inhospitable again, and one can understand the complaints of the Israelites as they journeyed through the desert and needed water. In this desert, they came to bitter waters (Marah), which the Lord directed Moses to transform into sweet water by throwing a tree into the spring (Exod 15:22–25).

From this point, the **visitor** to the Sinai travels north along the Gulf of Suez and then **along the Suez Canal** to Port Tewfik or some other place along the Canal where the crossing of the canal takes place en route to **Cairo**.

The Israelites in their journey into the Sinai **after the Passover** night, which saw the death of the firstborn Egyptians, **left Rameses and the land of Goshen** and traveled south in Egypt to **Succoth** which was located just north of the Bitter Lakes that served as an Egyptian barrier to invaders (Exod 12:37). Then, rather than attempting to cross near the string of fortresses that protected Egypt, in a strange twist the Israelites apparently **turned north** again to Pihahithroth near Migdol and Baal-zephon which caught the **attention of the Pharaoh,** who decided to pursue them with his chariot forces (Exod 14:1–7). Under the guidance of God, the Israelites then crossed miraculously on dry land into the Sinai probably through the northern marshes or lakes called **Yam Suph**, which does *not* mean—as sometimes supposed—the **Red Sea**, but probably means something like the **Sea of Reeds**, or **Sea of Weeds**. After the Israelites successfully crossed beyond this marshy sea, the water then returned to the deep marshes, the Egyptian chariots became bogged down in the muddy waters, and the returning tides engulfed Pharaoh and his forces and they died in the flood (Exod 14:13–31).

25. The dock for crossing the Suez Canal

And so it is time to enter the main part of Egypt.

IX

VISITING EGYPT

For many people, a visit to Egypt comes very close to their goal of visiting Israel. When they think of Ancient Egypt, the Pyramids and the Sphinx come immediately to mind. While these monuments are very significant symbols of Egypt, there is in fact much more for the visitor to see in Egypt.

THE LAND OF EGYPT
(The Eastern Section)

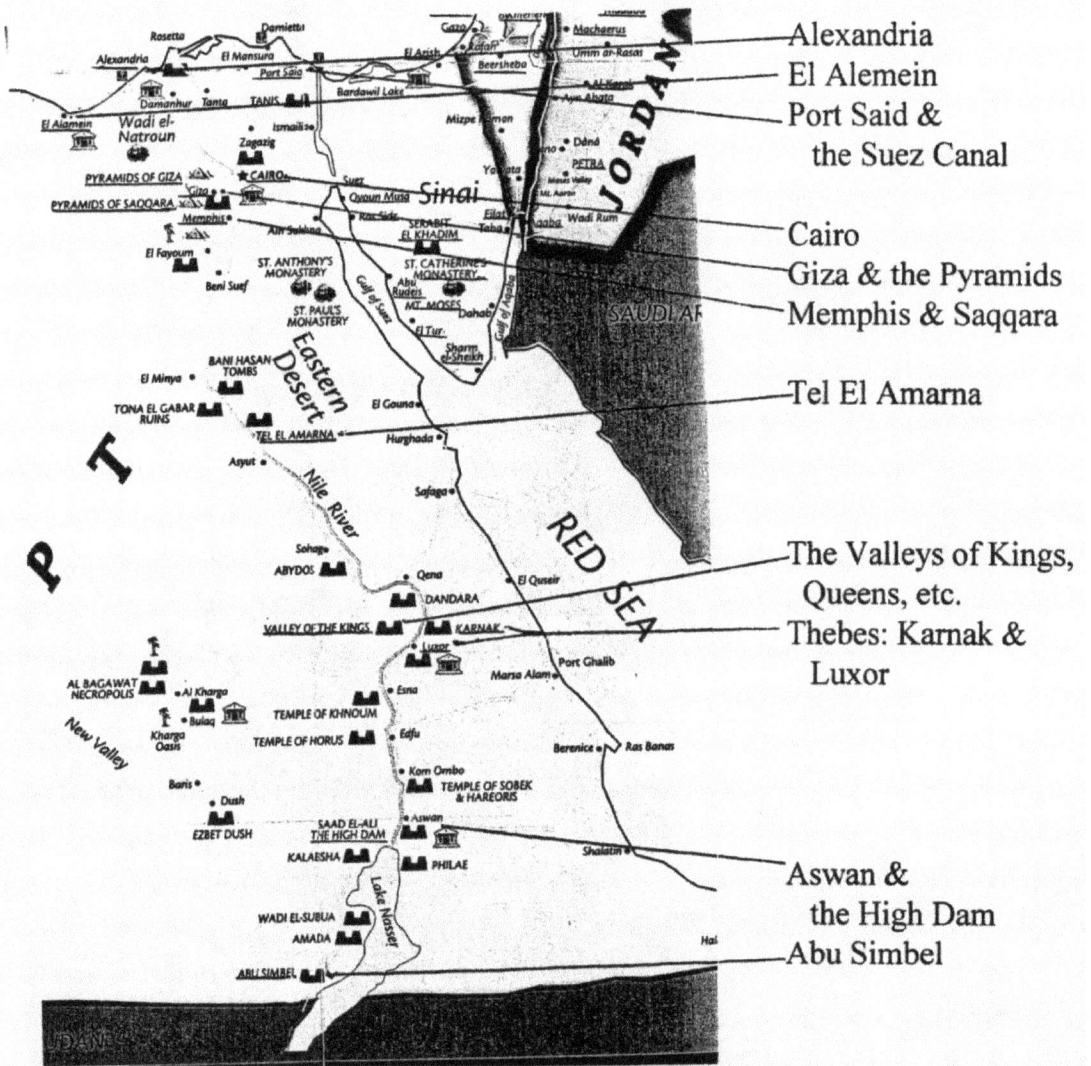

- Alexandria
- El Alemein
- Port Said & the Suez Canal
- Cairo
- Giza & the Pyramids
- Memphis & Saqqara
- Tel El Amarna
- The Valleys of Kings, Queens, etc.
- Thebes: Karnak & Luxor
- Aswan & the High Dam
- Abu Simbel

GENERAL INFORMATION ABOUT EGYPT

In reflecting on Egypt, one could easily conclude, as the Greek writer Herodotus stated, that Egypt's importance has resulted from "the **gift of the Nile.**" Egypt is dependent on the Nile River, and in more recent years one could add the Suez Canal as well. Indeed, ninety-nine percent of its population lives near the Nile or the Canal. The rest of Egypt is basically a non-inviting desert. Egypt has the **largest population in the Arab alliance** of over seventy million, and one-seventh of them live in or near Cairo. Accordingly, modern cities like **Cairo** are exceedingly compact and densely populated. While Egypt is a modern state, many people are still poor and even live in temporary housing or in the cemeteries (tomb shelters), as they eke out their livelihood.

The name Egypt is a transliterated form of the Greek word *Aigyptos* which was derived from the name of the principal temple *ha(t)kaptah* in the ancient capital of Memphis. As will be indicated below, Egypt became a powerful force in the Mediterranean world when King Menes of Upper Egypt (south of the Delta) conquered Lower Egypt and united the two regions sometime after 3100 B.C. The capital of the united kingdom was later established at **Memphis.** Following the union of the two regions, there was a great **stimulus for advancement**, and the farmers, who had earlier recognized the importance of the Nile, developed new strategies for harnessing the nutrients of the river by forming catch basins in their lands that captured the rich soil carried by the Nile during its flood stages.

As the **Old Kingdom** emerged, artisans were encouraged to pursue stone carving and painting as priests and others sought to understand the meaning of life and death and depict these realities. Medical advancements were made through men like **Imhotep**, and new concepts of burying the dead were also developed. In succeeding years, Egypt became a major force in the Mediterranean world, and during biblical times it **vied with the countries of Mesopotamia** for dominance until Macedonia and later Rome became the world powers. Even though Egypt slipped from its dominant role in world politics, the religion of **Isis and Osiris** became known in many other parts of the Mediterranean area.

The Coptic Christian tradition is that Mark, the evangelist, came to Egypt in the year A.D. 61 and in spite of persecution, Christianity took a firm root in Egypt. By the end of the fourth century Christianity became the official religion of Egypt. The building of churches began in earnest in the fifth century. In A.D. 451, Christian theologians reached a great divide in theology over the nature of Jesus Christ. To quote Father Bestavros of Abu Sarga—the oldest church in Egypt—from the Coptic point of view, the Western and Greek Church argued that Jesus maintained two natures while the Copts, the Armenians, and the Syrians maintained "that out of the two natures there arose one single Nature." The former then accused the latter of the "heresy of Eutechius" and the latter accused the former of 'the heresy of Nestorius." The war of words created a division that still continues to the present between the east and the west.

During the Byzantine period both Christian and non-Christian **asceticism** and monasticism found a welcome home in the dry desert settings of Egypt. The **Coptic** language in its various dialects (including Sahidic and Boharic) was spoken, and ancient documents, which have been found well-preserved in the dry climate of Egypt, were transcribed here. Indeed, the sands at Nag Hammadi in Upper Egypt gave up scores of ancient speculative Coptic Gnostic documents in the twentieth century, some of which I worked on during my doctoral studies.

In the seventh century, Egypt yielded to the advance of the military forces of **Islam** under the Arabs. Churches were destroyed, and many Christians were forced on pain of death to convert to Islam. Other Christians were allowed to live, but Christianity was reduced to a minority religion in what became known as the **Millet system**, which permits no proselytism out of Islam. The Fatimites controlled Egypt from 969 to 1171 and developed Cairo into a major Muslim city. They were followed by the Ayyubids [1171–1250], who were inspired by the powerful Saladin, the victor over the Crusaders. They yielded to Mamelukes in 1250, who in turn were conquered by the powerful **Ottoman Turks** in 1517. The common language is now Arabic.

Napoleon invaded Egypt in 1798, and a combined force of British and Ottomans then defeated the French in 1801. The long anticipated **modern Suez Canal** was completed with British assistance in 1869, and the Egyptian monarchy sold Egypt's partnership rights to the Canal to the British in 1875. The Allies gave **Britain a Protectorate** status over Egypt in 1914 that the British relinquished in 1922.

After the failed attempt of the Arab countries to eliminate Israel and the Jews from Palestine in 1948, the **military** (the Free Officers) **overthrew the monarchy** (King Farouk) on July 23, 1952, and **established Egypt as a republic** in 1953. Britain then agreed to give up control of the Suez Canal in 1956, but Gamel Abdel **Nasser** was **elected pres-**

ident in June of that year, which led the United States and Great Britain to withdraw assistance in building the Aswan Dam. Then Egypt attacked Israel, and the **Israelis** responded by invading Egypt and **capturing the Sinai**. When Egypt refused to withdraw from the Canal Zone, a brief war with Britain, France, and Israel ensued; however, it was quickly terminated by the United Nations, and Britain and France left Egypt. The **Aswan Dam** was constructed with the assistance of the Soviets in 1960 and **completed in 1968**. After a few battles between Israel and Egypt, a **peace treaty** was signed between Egypt and Israel and the **Sinai was returned** to Egypt in 1979.

TABLE 9.1

CHRONOLOGY OF ANCIENT EGYPT

Because early Egyptian history is both **defined in terms of dynasties** and **rather complex**, I herewith present readers with a brief outline of the dynasties. I have **highlighted** what generally are regarded as the important events for readers, visitors to museums and pilgrims to Egypt.

APPROXIMATE DATES	PERIOD	DYNASTY AND IMPORTANCE
(Prior to) 3100 B.C.	(Neolithic Period) Thinite Rule	· *Namer/Menes united Upper and Lower Egypt.* · Dynasty I—Capital: Abydos/Thinis in Upper Egypt. · *Union of the Red Crown of the north to the tall White Crown of the south.* · Heliopolis, along with Nekheb, regarded as sacred cities of the priests. Aha founded Memphis.
2850–2775	Thinite Rule (cont'd.)	· Dynasty II—Capital: Memphis in Lower Egypt. · *Heliopolis* center of religious authority.
2775–2180	*Old Kingdom*	· **Dynasties III–VI.** In this period, *art and architecture reached a zenith.* Capital: Memphis. · III—*Sakkara: Step pyramid built by Zoser.* · IV—[2620–2500] **GREAT PYRAMIDS** *built by Cheops, Kafre, and Menkaure.* · V—*Sahure digs* **FIRST CHANNEL** from Red Sea to the Mediterranean. · *Unas* builds his pyramid and funerary temple; contains the important *Pyramid Texts* and the

		Wisdom of Ptah-Hotep; among the oldest religious texts in the world. · VI—Central power collapses with Pepi II.
2180–2000	A Transition Period	· VII–XI—Feuds among the ruling classes; Capitals: Memphis, Abydos, Heracleopolis (Middle Egypt), and Thebes (Upper Egypt). · XI—Reestablishment of central authority from Upper Egypt to Lower Egypt. Restoration of trade along caravan routes and on the sea.
2000–1780	Middle Kingdom	· **Dynasty XII**—Feudal Rulers from Thebes unite Egypt. · Expanded power south beyond 3rd Cataract to middle of the Sudan and along the coast to Megiddo and Ugarit.
1780–1745		· Dynasty XIII—Weak rulers followed by destabilization.
1745–1580	**Hyksos Period**	· **XIV–XVII *SHEPHERD KINGS*—**Canaanites and Ammonites used chariot forces to take control of Egypt. · ***PROBABLE TIME for JOSEPH in Egypt.*** · XIV—Introduction of ***BAAL WORSHIP into Egypt.*** · XV—Capital: Avaris. ***Upper Egypt rebeled*** and defeated Apophis and the Hyksos. · XVI—Capital: Thebes. Kamose rebeled in Middle Egypt against Hyksos. Ahmose reconquers Nubia to Abu Simbel. · XVII—Weak Hyksos rule in Lower Egypt.
1580–1310	New Kingdom	· *A strong Egypt emerges.* **Dynasty XVIII established.** · Capitals: Thebes (and Akhetaten). · Thutmose I: [1530–1520] **rebuilt the *Temple of Karnak*** as well as the cities of Thebes and Abydos. · Thutmose II [1520–1505] married half-sister Hatshepsut. · *HATSHEPSUT* [1505–1484] *ruled Egypt as a male regent* for her son. · *THUTMOSE III* [1484–1450]; *one of the **most famous warrior pharoahs**,* defeated the Syrians, the Mitanni, also extended Egyptian rule over the Greek islands so that *EGYPTIAN CULTURE*

became *DOMINANT* throughout the Mediterranean world.

· *AMENOPHIS IV* [1370–1354] *changed his name to AKHENATEN.* He replaced the worship of Amon Ra (the sun god) with a *MONOTHEISTIC religion of ATEN* in which *all people were regarded as equal* and the pharaoh was understood not as a "god" but as a human prophet. *New capital at Akhenaten. Married Mitannian princess named Nefertiti,* who was regarded as "the beautiful one."

· Tutankhaten/*TUTANKHAMUN* [1354–1345] ruled under the regency of Nefertiti until the priests succeeded in convincing him to *return to the worship of AMON.* The reason for his death at eighteen continues to be disputed.

· After her son's death, *Nefertiti continued* to exert authority in Egypt until 1340 by marrying old Ay, but then she was supplanted and her tomb has been lost or purposely destroyed.

· *HOREMHEB* [1340–1314], a former friend of Akenaten and a shrewd general, *rejected the worship of Aten* and forefully destroyed almost all evidence of Akhenaten, declaring a *curse on him* and his religion.

1314–1200	New Kingdom (cont'd.)	· **Dynasty XIX**—Capitals: Tanis and Thebes. · *PROBABLE TIME OF THE EXODUS.* (Ramesses I [1314–1312] chose new capital at Tanis. Viewed himself as "prince of the whole earth.") · *RAMESSES II* [1298–1235]—*EGYPT'S LEADING PHARAOH* developed a major army and defeated the Hittites at Kadesh, but with the growing threat from their common enemy, the Assyrians, he agreed to a *historic peace treaty* with the Hittites under the watchful eye of Re (the god of Thebes) and Teshub (the god of Hattusa).
1200–1088	New Kingdom (cont'd.)	· **Dynasty XX**—Capital: Thebes · Ramesses III [1198–1188] sought to correct weaknesses in the kingdom and end the incursions of the sea peoples along the coast.
1090–945	A Transition Period	· XXI—Fierce feuds among priests and nobility. · Egypted fragmented into small fiefdoms.

950–730	**Libyan Period**	· Dynasties XXII–XXIII—Capital: Bubasitis. · *SHISHAK I*/*Sheshonq* [950–929] founded Dynasty XXII by conquering Egypt from Libya. *Swept into Judah and Israel, breeching the fortresses of Solomon.*
750–670	Sudanese/Ethiopian Period	· Dynasties XXIV-XXV—Piankhi [751–716] over-threw theLibyans. Capitals: Sais and Napata, then Thebes. · Bocchorus [720–716] negotiates temporary peace with Assyrians. · Egyptian annals indicate that *SHABATAKA* [701–689] *squelched a revolt on the part of Hezekiah that is **NOT** recorded in our biblical texts.* Nevertheless, this pharaoh was defeated by Sennacherib.
670	**Assyrian Conquest**	· The Mesopotamians then flexed their muscles over a weak Egypt. Dynasty XXVI—Capital: Sais. · Neco I [670–663] conspires with Assyria and assumes power in Egypt. His son, Psamtik I [663–609] makes alliances with Greeks to **free Egypt from Assyria**. · *NECO II* [609–594] recognized the rise of Babylon and aligned with Assyria to counter the new power. As he marched north, *JOSIAH of JUDAH tried to stop him at Megiddo but was killed* [609]. Neco **rebuilt the canal** from the Red Sea to the Mediterranean for trade.
525	**Persian Conquest**	· **Dynasty XXVII**—Capitals: Sais and Memphis. · *CAMBYSES* [525–522] *the son of Cyrus,* finally conquered Egypt and was **confirmed as a pharaoh** at Heliopolis. North Africa as far as Libya was brought into the Achaemenid Empire.
525	Quest for Independence	· Dynasties XXVIII–XIX—Capitals: Sais and Mendes. · Achoris [390–378] rebuilds the Egyptian fleet and aligns Egypt with Greeks against Persia. · Dynasty XXX [378–333]—Persia reasserts control over Egyptian capitals: Sebennytus and Memphis.
333	**The Greek Period**	· *ALEXANDER* [333–323] defeated the Persians and was *welcomed as a hero in Egypt*. Acknowledged as the successor to the pharaohs. *Recognized as the*

		son of Ra at Luxor. Founded Alexandria. Died in Babylon. His body brought to Egypt by Alexander's general, Ptolemy, who agreed with the other generals to split Alexander's kingdom.
311	**PTOLEMAIC PERIOD**	Capital: Alexandria. After a period of indecisiveness in Macedonia, Ptolemy I Soter [306–285] assumed the role of ruler in Egypt. Built Ptolemais near Thebes, which lay in ruins, and seized Palestine from Seleucus, contrary to the earlier agreement of the generals that led to the *continued BATTLES BETWEEN SELEUCIDS AND PTOLEMIES dscribed in Daniel 11.* · *Ptolemy II Philadelphus* [285–246] expanded Greek culture in Egypt. Built the famous lighthouse and, as Jewish tradition suggests, encouraged the translation of the Hebrew Bible into the **Greek Septuagint (LXX)**.
167ff.	*Roman Involvement*	· Started when Antiochus IV of Syria invaded Egypt. Rome stepped into the picture. · *Julius Caesar married Cleopatra VII* [the sister of Ptolemy XIII Neo Dionysos]. Caesar was recognized as a pharaoh and a *son of Amon*. They envisioned an empire ruled by Rome and Egypt. · Murder of Caesar [44 B.C.] left Cleopatra bereft. She enticed Mark Antony to plan for a similar goal. · Cleopatra and Mark Antony defeated by Octavian [later Augustus] at Actium in 31 B.C. Egypt was made a Roman province. · Rome continued its influence in Egypt through the Byzantine period.
A.D. 639–642ff.	*The Muslim Period*	· The Arabs conquered Egypt and forcefully turned it to Islam. Christianity permitted only as a minority religion, and prosyletism was forbidden.

The Pyramid Period

The **Old Kingdom** (2775–2180 B.C.) was a great period of building, and many pyramids were constructed throughout the land. Near the old capital of Memphis lies **Sakkara**, where the **Step Pyramid of Zoser** and his funerary temple are located. Near Sakkara is also the **Pyramid of Unas**, with its *Pyramid Texts*, which are some of the oldest preserved religious records in existence. Of course, every visitor to Egypt expects to see the **three great pyramids at Giza** that today are encompassed within the greater environs of Cairo. As an indication of how fast Cairo is growing, when I first visited Egypt in the sixties these pyramids were some distance away from the city.

The **largest of the pyramids** at Giza is the one that honors **Cheops**, or **Kufu**, the most revered monarch of the Fourth Dynasty. He **inspired 100,000 Egyptian young men** to join in the construction of his monument that contains **2.5 million blocks of limestone** so well-engineered that a razor blade hardly fits between the stones. This construction feat involved a superb understanding of algebra and geometry and included a highly developed sense of astrology (an amazing understanding of the movements of heavenly bodies). When Cheops died, he was ceremonially buried in the tomb.[1]

Climbing the **narrow shaft** of the pyramid to the **interior vault** is an intriguing experience for those who do not become claustrophobic. But reaching the chamber can be a slight disappointment for those who might expect to find a sarcophagus in it, because these have been removed and there is nothing much to be seen inside the burial site.

26. The Sphinx and the pyramid of Chefren

---

1. Visitors to the pyramids should remember that a pyramid in Semitic thinking is a precise combination of the numbers 3 (representing the divine) and 4 (representing the flat earth), a testimony to the Egyptian view that the tomb of a **pharaoh** belongs to a person who **embodied both realities of the human and the divine.**

The **second** of the great pyramids belonged to **Kafre** or **Chefren**, the son of Cheops, who purposely made his structure a little smaller in honor of his father. The smooth slabs at the summit are all that now remain of the smooth **casing** that once covered the pyramid, giving it a glistening appearance in the sun. The **third** pyramid belonged to **Menkau'ra**, or **Mycernius**, who followed his father's example of constructing his tomb a little smaller than the second. The effect created a fascinating triad of memorials.

In front of and below Chefren's Pyramid is the **Great Sphinx**, which was constructed with the face in the likeness of Chefren. The Temple was an intricate part of the large **necropolis** ("city of the dead") in which queens, nobles, and other citizens of rank were buried to support the pharaoh in his journey to the afterlife. The Sphinx memorial had two aisles of granite pillars in front of which were a series of statues of the pharaoh in various crowns. In **contrast** to the usual Egyptian representation of the **gods**, which were portrayed with the **head of a bird or an animal and the body of a human**, the sphinx is portrayed with the **body of a lion and the head of a human**. The reason for its deface-ment is due to the Mamelukes, who used the Sphinx as a target for their cannon practice. A false beard, which later became typical of Egyptian monarchs, was added to the Sphinx by Thutmose IV and is now in the Egyptian Museum.

Along the **Nile plateau there are at least thirty-eight pyramids** that were con-structed from the head of the plateau at Abu Roash through Giza to the great grouping in the vicinity of **Sakkara** (**Saqqara**) and as far south as El-Lahun. The earliest pyramids are from the Third Dynasty (Neferke and Khaba at Zawiyat al-Aryan, and Sekhemket and the well-known Step Pyramid of Zoser at Sakkara—all **south of Giza**). The famous Pyramid of Unas with the important *Pyramid Texts* from the Fifth Dynasty is also at Sakkara. After the Sixth Dynasty the pharaohs were buried elsewhere, primarily south in the **Valley of the Kings**, but in the **Twelfth Dynasty** ten rulers from the powerful time of the Middle Kingdom returned to building pyramids on the plateau further south of Sakkara.

Approaching the Various Areas in Egypt

Visitors to Egypt will normally use buses, trains, airplanes, and boats in reaching the various areas and sites of Egypt near the Nile River because the narrow strip of habitable land along the Nile in Egypt's segment of the river from the Sudan to the Mediterranean Sea stretches for about 960 miles as it flows north (which is just under a quarter of the Nile's total journey of nearly 4,200 miles through northeastern Africa). While there are countless sites that could be visited in Egypt, I have selected a number for special attention in this book that should provide a stimulating sampling of the wonders of Egypt.

THE REGION OF ALEXANDRIA AND THE NORTH OF EGYPT

Alexander the Great founded **Alexandria** in 331 B.C. on the northwest edge of the Nile Delta and on the site of an older harbor protected by the island of Pharos in the Mediterranean. Since there were very few adequate harbors for trade besides the Phoenician ports, Alexander recognized the strategic significance of this site. But it was his general, **Ptolemy I Soter**, that became the ruler of Egypt after the death of Alexander, and who in fact began to realize the dream of Alexander by building a **causeway** from the mainland to the island; thus, he created **twin significant harbors** that were connected by a bridge system. As indicated above, the famous **Lighthouse**, which was one of the great wonders of the world, was built here during the reign of Ptolemy II Philadelphus, who also encouraged the significant Jewish population to translate the Hebrew Bible into Greek (the Septuagint, or LXX). The great **Library of Euclid**, founded by Demetrios of Phaleron, was also located here. Tragically, in **48 B.C.** during the Roman siege of Alexandria by **Julius Caesar**, the great **library** was **destroyed**, and later the great **lighthouse** fell into the sea during an **earthquake**. Divers have since been combing the sea for remnants of the ancient city, which is mostly **underwater.** Christians developed the *Didaskaleion* (an important catechetical school) here in the second century before the severe persecution of the later emperors erupted.

Today, visitors to Egypt's second largest city can gain entrance to the catacombs and the Greco-Roman Museum, which houses a number of significant antiquities. Also, a visit to the site designated as **Pompey's Column** in the midst of other ruins is interesting. For those seeking respite from travel, the gardens and beaches on the banks of the Mediterranean at **Montazah Palace** are inviting. Besides the modern hotels, which dominate the shoreline and skyline of Alexandria, one should see the magnificent **Fortress of Qaitbay**.

Along the Mediterranean coast about four miles from land in the Bay of Abu Qir Egyptian, French and American marine archaeologists recently (2000) discovered the fabled city of Herakleion (named for Hercules), which the Greek historian Herodotus visited in 450 B.C. The city was a religious center for the Mysteries of Isis, Serapis, and the later Osiris and was a major seaport before the building of Alexandria. It apparently suffered from an earthquake in the seventh or eighth century A.D. and sank into the sea. Lead archaeologist F. Goddio indicated that homes and other buildings that were not damaged in the earthquake have been "frozen in time" by the water. Nearby were also found two other small cities named for two "immortals": Canopus (who was the helmsman for King Menelaus in the story of the return of Helen from Troy and who put in at Herakleion but was bitten by a snake and according to the legend became a "god"), and the other is named after his wife Menouthis.

Approximately an hour and one-half distance by bus, west from Alexandria along the coastal highway in the desert, is **El Alamein** where one of the fiercest battles of **World War II** took place between the Allied forces under British General Montgomery on the one hand and the German and Italian forces under German General Rommel on the other. Although the British were caught by surprise in the Axis goal of capturing the Suez Canal, they held firm at this point and ultimately pushed the Germans and Italians out of Egypt. The large cemeteries and the museum here provide a silent testimony to the necessity of pursuing peace instead of war in the conduct of international relations.

East of Alexandria, guarding the Mediterranean entrance to the Suez Canal, is the modern city of **Port Said**, which was the midpoint goal of the German forces in their quest to achieve complete control of the Mediterranean basin.

Opened in 1869, the **Suez Canal** extends approximately 100 miles from the north to the south, where it exits into the Gulf of Suez. It has no locks and has been the busiest such waterway in the world. It has been deepened and widened several times, but—save for the Al Ballah Bypass near the midpoint—most of the Canal allows only ships going in one direction at a time. In 1950, after the first Arab-Israeli war, Israeli ships were prevented from using this international waterway. During the 1967 Arab-Israeli War, it was closed because of sunken ships and was not reopened until 1975. After the peace accord was signed between Israel and Egypt in 1979, Israeli ships were again permitted to use the Canal. In 1980, a tunnel was completed under the Canal near the southern end of the waterway and the city of Suez for the direct access of motor vehicles to the Sinai.

In 1975, Israeli aerial photographers confirmed the existence of a **much earlier waterway** (as described in the ancient Egyptian annals) now covered by the sands, which began at **Pelusium** (east of Port Said on the Mediterranean), running in a southwesterly direction crossing the current Canal, proceeding south to the current city of Isamalia, then surprisingly **splitting** and following the Wadi Tumilat to the **Nile River** with the other branch continuing south to the **Gulf of Suez**. Then the archaeologists on the ground confirmed that the waterway was dug to a depth of between seven and ten feet—sufficient for Egyptian barges of that time—but as wide as 200 feet in places, obviously intended as a barrier to invaders. The brilliant Egyptians who were able to build the pyramids were also able to construct a great canal system.

THE REGION OF CAIRO

A Brief History of Cairo

Mention has already been made of the fact that Cairo is the megapolis of Egypt that is literally swallowing the surrounding territory. Prior to A.D. 970 and its founding, the site was basically a town in the desert.

A few **interesting legends** are associated with its location. The first involves the Arab commander **Amr Ibn El-As**, who invaded Egypt in A.D. 640. As he was chasing the Romans to a nearby fortress, they destroyed the bridge crossing the Nile; so he camped at **El Fostat**. After vanquishing the local Roman military, he returned to camp and prepared to move on to Alexandria. But a **pair of pigeons** apparently had made a nest at the top of the tent with some eggs in it, so he left his tent and continued on his mission. After conquering Alexandria, he returned to the site and built a house, a barracks for his troops, and the first mosque in Egypt. With such a beginning, the mosque became revered and served as a site for prayers, especially when it seemed as though the waters of the Nile would not flood and local farmers would not be able to produce food. As the town grew, it was **divided into quadrants**, including one for the Arabs, another for the Romans, and a third for the Jews. The Christian Copts clustered in a section where some earlier churches and a monastery had been located. Another disputed legend has circulated that Ibn El-As put an end to the tradition that a **virgin girl was sacrificed yearly** to the Nile so that an adequate flood would be forthcoming to ensure plentiful crops.

In the **ninth century** during the reign of Ahmed Ibn Tulun, the town was expanded to the hill on which a citadel was located. It had wells and some canals to provide water for the residents, and a mosque was constructed in his honor. Then in the **tenth century** the **Fatimids** who conquered Egypt desired to establish a major city that would **vie in importance with Baghdad**, the city of the Abbassides, their Muslim **competitors**. Thus was born Al-Kahira, or Cairo. Gohar El-Sakly, the Fatimite commander, was placed in charge of building the great city. Among the initial important buildings constructed were the **Al-Azhar Mosque** and the **Manesterly Palace**. A great wall with a number of gates surrounded the city. The most famous of these are the **Bab Al-Nasr**, named for the king who entered the city victoriously after defeating the Tartars in approximately 1290, and **Bab El-Fetouh**, through which Selim I and the Ottomans entered in 1517 and through which Napoleon also rode in 1798.

Seeing Some of the Important Sites in Cairo

A must among the most important sites to visit in Cairo is the **world famous Egyptian Museum**, which would take several days to view the vast number of archaeological treasures that are on display, to say nothing of those that are in storage. Here are the **treasures of Tutankhamun**, some of which have been exhibited in various cities of the world. In the main hall is the magnificent seated statue of **Amenophis III with his wife** that is nearly **thirty-five feet high**! Here also are several items from the unique reign of Akhenaten found at Karnak, including a sandstone sculpture of **Akhenaten** and a quartzite **head of Nefertiti**. And here you will find a granite statue of **Hatshepsut**, the woman who dared to become a pharaoh, with her false beard. All of these items are from the Eighteenth Dynasty. But you will also find a black dolomite statue of **Khafre** with the falcon god Horus from the Third Dynasty and the sculpture of a working scribe from the Fourth Dynasty. The archaeological treasures are far too many to mention.

One also cannot visit Egypt without seeing **statues**—whether they are original or copies—of **Ramesses II** with the double crown of the united kingdom, one of the symbols of Egypt. Among the most impressive of these treasures are the **two gigantic statues** about forty-three feet in height that were recovered from the sands at Memphis, the former capital of Egypt. One in excellent condition was brought to the modern capital of Cairo and set up in the main station square; the other, fractured one remains lying in the sand at the old capital surrounded by a platform for viewing the statue. This pharaoh (considered Egypt's preeminent ruler) fathered at least 200 children during his long reign of sixty-three years, and among the many attributes given to him was the designation "the strong ox."

27. The Mohammad Ali Mosque in Cairo

Among the scores of important mosques to visit, mention should be made of the **Mohammad Ali Mosque**, which was built in 1830 and modeled on the historic Hagia Sophia (the former Christian cathedral) in Constantinople/Istanbul. Rings of chandeliers illuminate this copy of the great dome and provide a slightly smaller representation of what was once the largest building in the Byzantine period. Also impressive is the **Mosque of Sultan Hassan**, which was constructed in the fourteenth century. An even earlier representative of Islamic architecture is the **Mosque of Ibn Tulun** from the ninth century.

On Mokattam hill, the magnificent **Cairo Citadel** was planned in 1174 by **Saladin El-Ayoubi** not for warfare but as a place for his residence, because he viewed it as having cleaner air than elsewhere. As the **story** goes, **meat would last here for two days** instead of one in the rest of Cairo. But before he could begin the building, he departed to counter the Crusaders incursion into Palestine, so the work was left to Bahaeddin Karakoush, his chief minister, who was a cruel taskmaster.

Many stories have circulated concerning the foibles of Karakoush, who was hated by the citizens of Cairo. Among the tales was his endeavor to gain more water from the Citadel well by enlarging it, but the water turned salty instead. Another involved a man who upon seeing a beautiful woman in a red dress lost his balance and fell off the city wall. Like the rabbinic stories in which a rabbi blamed a beautiful young woman for causing his students to misdirect their attention from their studies, Karakoush had the woman seized and pronounced her death, whereupon she blamed the merchant who sold her the red dress! Karakoush immediately condemned him, and he in turn blamed the dyer for the red color. But the dyer was too tall to fit the gallows, so Karakoush hung another dyer instead! The **Citadel was finally completed in 1219** by Saladin's nephew, and it was built with grand marble columns and contained fine carpets and ornaments, which the Turks later removed to Istanbul.

Among the Christian sites of some importance is the **church** dedicated to the **Flight of the Holy Family**. At Mataria, a church has been built because of a **legend** suggesting there was **a tree** at the site that provided shelter for the family in their flight from King Herod. A small pond there is said to be the place where the baby **Jesus was bathed**. But more to the point is the fact that the Church of Abu Sarga (St. Sagius) is dedicated to the memory of martyrs Sargious and Bachus who were killed on October 7, 296. The church has twelve pillars for the twelve apostles—eleven are painted, but one is dull and almost **black for Judas** the traitor. Also of interest is the modern tradition of the **Virgin Mary appearance** in the belfry of the Coptic Orthodox church of Zeitoun in **1968**. After the late Coptic Patriarch Ambra Kyrillos "confirmed" the event as an authentic miracle, visitors from many places began pilgrimages to the site.

The large modern **Marcossia Cathedral** at Abbassia houses excellent examples of Coptic art and provides an interesting stop for the visitor. It is the largest cathedral in Africa and now contains relics from St. Mark that were reportedly taken by a sailor in the **ninth century** to Venice and buried there in the Basilica of St. Mark. Negotiations between Coptic Patriarch Kyrillos and Rome arranged to have the relics **returned to Egypt**.

The Environs of Cairo

Within the environs of modern Cairo are the cities of Giza and Heliopolis. Attention has already been given to **Giza** in the **discussion of the Pyramids** and the Nile Plateau.

Heliopolis is the Greek name for the city of the **Sun god "Ra"** (or **Re**). The worship of Re developed primarily in Lower Egypt (the north) in connection with the capital at Memphis, and Re was considered to be the god of all the living, just as **Osiris** and his wife **Isis** were viewed as the gods of the dead. Among other members of the **Egyptian godhead or pantheon** are **Set** (the evil brother of Osiris) and his wife **Nephthys; Shu**, the god of the air; **Nut**, the goddess of the sky; **Geb**, the god of the earth; and **Tetnut**, the goddess of moisture. But **Re**, or **Ra**, was primary and was pictured in Egyptian art with a **human body and the head of a falcon**. In the worship of Re, the priests at Heliopolis developed the first state religion, and the pharaohs were confirmed as **sons of Re** at Heliopolis. As the thinking developed, Re became viewed as the god of the whole world. The final step taken by Akhenaten was the beginning of Egyptian monotheism in the religion of **Aten** (see Tel el-Amarna, below), a god who was pictured merely as a sun disk, but Akhenaten's views were forcibly rejected by the succeeding pharaohs and their priests.

Virtually nothing remains of the ancient city and the temple complex at Heliopolis. In modern times, the area was basically a desert, until a Belgian entrepreneur, Baron Empain, developed an electric transportation system and built villas, parks and casinos. **Today**, Heliopolis is a thriving large city within the Cairo metroplex.

THE REGION OF MEMPHIS AND SAQQARA (SAKKARA)

Almost nothing remains today of the Old Capital of **Menufer**, or **Memphis** in Greek, which was founded in the last part of Dynasty I and probably was originally designed by Imhotep, who was also a brilliant medical scientist. It was rebuilt and expanded several times during the centuries, ultimately succumbing to ruin during the establishment and growth of Alexandria. The stones of its temples and other structures were pirated for secondary use by later builders in Cairo and elsewhere.

28. One of two statues of Ramesses II found at Memphis

Archaeologists working in the area of Memphis in the nineteenth century came upon a few remains from the illustrious **Temple of Ptah** in which the pharaohs where crowned. Among the discoveries were **two statues of Ramesses II** (Nineteenth Dynasty, commonly regarded as Egypt's greatest Pharaoh), one of which was taken to Cairo. These statues originally were part of the great entrance to the temple. As indicated earlier, the broken one, which originally reached about forty-three feet in height, remains at the site for visitors to view. Among the few other remnants of the bygone glory of Memphis are some fractured portions of seated statues and a very large alabaster carved **sphinx of Amenophis II** (Eighteenth Dynasty) that guarded the Temple.

Much more can be seen at the once large **necropolis** (city of the dead) at **Saqqara (Sakkara)**. Here is the **Pyramid of Unas** (the last Pharaoh of the Fifth Dynasty) with its restored mortuary temple where the famous *Pyramid Texts* were discovered. Here also is the earlier Step Pyramid of Zoser (Third Dynasty). More than a score of tombs with their pictured **mastabas** giving insights into life during the various dynasties are also here.

> A TOURING NOTE: Generally, **tours to Memphis and Saqqara** visit only the sites of the fallen statue of Ramesses and the Step Pyramid, as well as a visit to a carpet making establishment, which may be a little disappointing to those whose appetites have been stimulated by a visit to the Egyptian Museum and might wish for a more intense encounter with the past and the giant necropolis at Saqqara. But others who are concerned with shopping might be more satisfied. Seeing more of the necropolis will necessitate special arrangements.

THE REGION OF TEL EL-AMARNA

Midway between Memphis and Luxor, archaeologists discovered an important ancient historic city at Tel el-Amarna. Here **to their delight was uncovered the palace of Akhenaten,** the so-called "heretical pharaoh," that the later ancient pharaohs tried to blot from Egyptian memory and history. Unlike the other palaces that proclaimed the grandeur and divinity of the pharaoh, the palace of Akhenaten bespeaks the **humanness and community-mindedness of the pharaoh.** Naturally the palace was situated above the other homes of citizens and was located on the king's road. Beyond a modest three-tiered garden, the palace complex does not however appear to have been sumptuous. It was constructed with a courtyard having rooms attached for the children and a main bedroom complex for the king and queen, which included a study for his painting and writing and a bathroom. The entire building was decorated with figures of domestic animals and birds, indicating a close attachment of its inhabitants to the physical world.

Here, a family from the powerful Eighteenth Dynasty lived out Egypt's first attempt at a **monotheistic religion** in which the **pharaoh did not regard himself as divine**. Here, Nefertiti and Amenophis IV—who changed his name to Akhenaten ("one pleasing to Aten")—must have sought to teach their children about the mystical view of "the Horizon of Aten," which reflected a very different concept of god and the pharaoh than was proclaimed in previous and later generations. But their son, who was named Tutankhaton, revised his name to Tutankhamun in honor of "Amon," the historic southern kingdom's designation for "the sun god," or the name "Amon Re," the united kingdom's name for the sun.

> **A Noteworthy Question**: In this context of monotheism and polytheism, the age-old question of good and evil raises its head. That question of why do the evil prosper and the good suffer confronts us periodically in varying contexts or situations. There is, of course, no easy answer as the book of Job made it very clear. Nevertheless, we are repeatedly forced to ponder that question of "Why?" We could hardly argue that Akhenaten was perfect, but was not his view of deity at least a little better than his successors? Why then did not his view of the world prevail? The answer can only be found in the death and resurrection of Jesus and not in the complexities of the present world or its politics.

THE REGION OF THEBES (KARNAK AND LUXOR) AND THE NEARBY VALLEY TOMBS (KINGS, QUEENS, NOBLES, AND WORKERS)

A pilgrim coming to visit Egypt should not fail to spend the time and extra money to travel south in order to ponder the great temples of Thebes, enter several tombs of the pharaohs with their magnificent painted pictorial stories, and gaze at the great memorial to Hatshepsut. It will be for that visitor a **never-to-be-forgotten experience**. I have returned again and again, and I have not lost my fascination for this part of Egypt. Lying about three hundred miles south of Cairo as the crow flies, one can take a night train, a flight in a small plane, or a cruise up the Nile to the small port in the little town of Luxor where one can overnight in one of the small hotels.

Less than two miles from the town of Luxor is **Karnak** in which is located the remains of the monumental **Temple of Amon**, dedicated to the principal god of Upper Egypt who at first was viewed as the god of air and fertility but later was united with Ra (or Re) from Lower Egypt and became the over-arching Sun god of the Egyptian Empire. The temple, with its hypostyle hall contains **138 gigantic columns** reaching approximately **seventy-five feet in height**, is breathtaking in its magnificence. Even though it is not set on a high plateau like the Parthenon in Athens or the Temple of Jupiter in Baalbek, it nevertheless is a magisterial monument from the past.

29. The Avenue of the Sphinxes at Karnak

Leading up to the first pylon (gate) are rows, or **avenues**, of protecting **ram-headed sphinxes**, which were the symbol of Amon. Inside the courtyard stands a huge **fifty-foot**

statue of Pinudjem, the high priest of Amon who became Pharaoh Tinita in the Twenty-first Dynasty. Around the court on the sides, one sees **statues of Ramesses III** in his ceremonial vestments. Beyond the courtyard is a Sacred Lake, constructed in the time of Amenophis III, the father of Akhenaten, and standing serenely in the area of carved pillars dedicated to Osiris stands the **Obelisk of Hatshepsut**. Around the lake are many fractured remains, including the **Obelisk of Amenophis III** with the sacred scarab (the symbol of renewed life), as well as other stone ruins. Two other small sanctuaries are also visible but are not dominating: one on the left to Montu and the other, on the right, to Mut.

Just outside the town of **Luxor** are the remains of the great **Temple of Amon Re**, which was originally built by Amenophis III, expanded by Thutmosis III, and further enhanced by Ramesses II. The Temple suffered severe damage during the conquest of Ashurbanipal (672 B.C.) and was further devastated during the period of the Ptolemies, who encountered resistance on the part of the Egyptians when they moved the capital to Alexandria. Later, during the Christian and Muslim eras, builders of churches and mosques used materials from the sites here in their construction projects. Archaeologists have since been able to reconstruct some parts of the great temple.

Flanking the entrance to the temple were originally rows of humanized sphinxes that led to **two large obelisks**, one of which is still present. Four large statues originally guarded the gateway, and archaeologists found **two of the four large seated statues of Ramesses II** that were apparently there. The entrance court of Ramesses can then be viewed leading to the three-sectioned **shrine of Thumose III**. Beyond the shrine is the aisle with **double columns topped by lotus buds**. Further into the complex is the great hall, which contains columns that rise approximately fifty-three feet in height and walls that were apparently **decorated by Tutankhamun** and **Horemheb**, who succeeded him. Among the inner sanctuaries is one that was established by **Alexander the Great** and one honoring the birth of **Amenophis III**. The surviving rows of pillars testify to the grandeur of the temple.

Visiting the **Valley of the Kings** and **Valley of the Queens** is a journey that is not only physical but should also be a journey into **reflection on views of the future**. Most of the pharaohs' grave sites have been **looted by grave robbers** who assured the world that the contents of those graves would not be transported into the afterlife of the owner as originally intended. The contents of one tomb (**Tutankhamun**) that did survive, however, give adequate testimony concerning the great wealth of the pharaohs who were buried in these tombs. The reason that "King Tut's stuff" remained to be found by those who opened his tomb in the modern period is probably due to the fact that his tomb was basically hidden, as it was located **beneath the tomb of Ramesses VI**.

But in spite of the fact that we are unable to access the physical contents of these twenty-two tombs that were found in the **Valley of the Kings**, visiting some of these tombs is a fascinating experience, because on the walls of many of the tombs are intriguing **hieroglyphic messages** and pictograms from the **Book of Dead**, as well as information concerning the former life of the occupant and each one's expectations concerning the future.

A visit should be made to nearby **Deir el-Bahri**, which is usually rendered the "Northern Monastery." This area, often improperly called Valley of the Queens, was dedicated to the **goddess Hathor** as early as the Eleventh Dynasty for use as a necropolis (city of the dead), but it was not used much until later. Reflecting on the impressive site and facing the mountain, one sees:

> (1) to the left, in this valley where **Montuhotep I** of the Eleventh Dynasty constructed a large necropolis with a small pyramid; (2) in the middle, where **Thutmose III** (the son of Hatshepsut and one of the greatest of the pharaohs) built a temple near the mountain, most of which no longer exists; and (3) to the right, the fascinating **Temple of Hatshepsut** (opposite page), designed by Setmut, her prime minister.

The Temple originally had an entrance avenue with sphinxes and obelisks, beyond which was a ramp leading to a second level in which the life and exploits of the queen-pharaoh were presented. Here also was a temple to Anubis, several chapels, and a temple to Hathor portrayed in the image of a cow. The third level up contained a shrine to Thutmose I (Hatshepsut's father) on the left, a sun temple to Harakhte on the right, and in the middle a memorial to Hatshepsut sacrificing a bull and an antelope. The paintings on the walls, once in brilliant colors, have now greatly faded, so what is mostly seen are the carved outlines of the pictograms.

Beyond this magnificent monument to Hatshepsut lies a desert valley that is properly known as the Valley of the Queens. At the entrance to the valley are several stellae offering prayers to Osiris and Anubis, as well as one enumerating the deeds of Ramesses

30. The Temple of Hatshepsut at Deir el-Bahri

III. In this valley about eighty tombs have been discovered, many of which have been desecrated and destroyed. Not only are queens buried here, but also some of their children, including royal princes. While the pictures in the princes' chambers are not as elaborate as those of the pharaohs, they are nonetheless done with great skill.

Near the Valley of the Queens are areas that were set aide for the Nobles and for the Workers. Since two of the three areas set aside for the nobles are basically on plains or flat ground and not up against a cliff as in the case of the pharaohs, these tombs are constructed with an entrance and set of steps leading down into the burial chamber. The other nearby area was set aside for the artisans who worked on the tombs. Even some of their tombs are beautifully decorated with pictograms and are worthy of a visit.

THE REGION OF ABU SIMBEL

THE REGION OF ABU SIMBEL

Moving much further south along the Nile, the visitor to Egypt reaches the **Aswan Dam** that created **Lake Nasser**, named in honor of Egypt's historic president who stood firmly for the independence of Egypt and for its place among contemporary nations of the world. The dam not only supplies **electrical power** for much of the nation but also is a means for controlling the **flood patterns of the Nile River.**

On the western bank of Lake Nasser near the boarder with Sudan and in the center of ancient Nubia lies Abu Simbel with **one of the most impressive monuments** erected to the memory of Ramesses II, who is generally regarded as the greatest of the Egyptian pharaohs. Here on the shores of the new lake are two sets each of two huge **seated statues of Ramesses** with an entrance to the cave like temple between them. The huge monument, which was referred to as *Ybsambul*, is carved into the side of the mountain with a facade measuring over **one hundred feet in height.** Over the centuries, it became mostly covered with the shifting sands and was basically forgotten until 1813, when parts of the heads and upper bodies were rediscovered. The **temple complex** was dedicated to the three gods Amon-Ra, Harmakhis, and Ptah, but Ramesses knew that the complex promoted his own importance as the pharaoh. The inscriptions in the temple recount his glorious activities, particularly the victory of Ramesses over the Hittites at Kadesh.

With the building of the dam, a **gigantic problem** ensued. In order to save the complex, it required that the entire fascade be taken apart by engineers and reassembled above the height of the lake. Accordingly, one could add that a second major feat was accomplished: not only was the original construction under the supervision of Pyay, the first directing sculptor, spectacular but so was the work of the twentieth century engineers who saved the magnificent artifact from a watery grave.

But there are some other important features to be noted. **Twice a year**, when the sun is at the correct position, **light** comes into the inner sanctuary where four smaller statues (three of the gods and one of Ramesses) are ensconced, and it shines upon Ramesses and the two gods Amon and Harmakhis but does not reach **Ptah, the deity of darkness.** Is this feature just a coincidence, or did the architect calculate it? What do you think?

The other matter concerns the fact that as one emerges from the temple cave, one comes upon the nearby **Temple of Hathor**, which Ramesses dedicated in honor of his favorite wife **Nofertari** (not to be confused with Neferteri/Nefertiti). In the history of the pharaohs, archaeologists have not found another example of a ruler building and dedicating a temple to one of his wives. **Ramesses** was a ruler that provided the world with interesting **surprises**!

MATTERS RELATED TO TRAVEL IN EGYPT AND THE SINAI[2]

Security Matters

Since the killing of several tourists in the region of Luxor and Karnak, Egyptian Security Forces have been placed on **continued alert to protect tourists**, especially those traveling in tour groups. Guides are either required to have a member of the security forces traveling with them, or their tour buses are monitored at each major crossing point in cities like Cairo. Whether travelers are aware of the fact or not, they may be more protected in Egypt and in a number of places in the Near East than they are in the United States of America. Even those who are **traveling by themselves** will be monitored as soon as they check into hotels.

Guides

Guides in Egypt are normally very knowledgeable about the history of sites. One of guides who spends time in the area of Luxor and Karnak has worked for the Egyptian Museum and can read the hieroglyphics, which is a great plus for those who have questions concerning the messages in the tombs and on the walls of the temples and monuments.

---

2. Readers are referred to comments made in a similar section on Israel.

Currency

What was said concerning the use of dollars in Israel applies also to Egypt, but having a few Egyptian pounds available for purchasing bottled water at local stores can be helpful, although merchants will generally accept dollars even though they may not know the current exchange rates.

WARNING: Concerning Eating Fresh Fruits, Vegetables, and Drinking Water

It is imperative to warn travelers **NOT TO EAT fresh fruits and vegetables** that cannot be peeled so as to avoid contracting stomach illnesses, unless one can be absolutely sure that they are free of contaminants. I give this **SERIOUS WARNING** because it is not fun being sick during travel.

Also, **DRINK ONLY BOTTLED WATER**, whether it is sparkling or still. Normal tap water in the hotels has **NOT been purified**, but water at restaurants in good hotels has normally been treated. Remember that this warning also applies to **brushing your teeth**. Be sure to check if you are in doubt!

X

ON THE ARAB-ISRAELI WARS AND THE PALESTINIAN REFUGEE PROBLEM: EGYPT, JORDAN, SYRIA, LEBANON, AND ISRAEL

Before I move on to a discussion of Jordan, it is imperative to make a brief excursus into the tragic situation involving the Palestinian refugees and their connection to the unrest in the Middle East.

When the **United Nations partitioned Palestine** in **1947**, the **Arab nations** refused to recognize the sovereignty of Israel and issued an **ultimatum to the Palestinians** to leave Israel or they would be eliminated along with the Jews. The war that followed in **1948** was a **disaster** for the Arab nations, especially for Jordan and Lebanon, both of whom had to contend with hundreds of thousands of refugees and whom they could not or would not integrate into their societies. The refugees were left in **makeshift camps** for years as a **symbol** of displaced persons for the world to see, and Israel refused to accept them back into the country. Having visited some of those camps in previous years, I sensed that a generation of young people was growing up **without hope**, which promised the coming of **radicalism** such as might not have been witnessed in the Middle East in previous generations.

In 1967, the **Six Day War** (which actually turned out to be three two-day wars in which Israel fought Egypt, then Syria, and finally Jordan separately) was an attempt on the part of the Arab nations to correct the 1948 loss. But it turned into an even **greater disaster** for the Arab nations, who lost more territory to Israel and did not solve the refugee problem. Briefly, I would note the following:

1. **Egypt lost** the **Sinai** to Israel, which has since been returned after the Egyptian-Israeli Accord was signed and Israel was permitted to reuse the Suez Canal. Has the problem with Egypt been solved? Partly! But the radical Palestinians in **Gaza** are on the border with Egypt in the Sinai, and their situation has hardly been resolved. The future is obviously not clear.

2. As a result of both wars and what followed, **Jordan lost** major access and control of **the West Bank** as the Palestinians continued to flood into Jordan. In an attempt to stop the influx, the **Jordanian troops attacked the Palestinian guerrillas** that were supporting the refugees in overrunning Jordan in September of 1970. In response and in support of the Palestinian forces, the **Syrians attacked the Jordanian military**, with their tanks and army creating an inter-Arab conflict; but in the same month they withdrew. Jordan has since relinquished

rights to the West Bank to the Palestinian Authority that must deal with Israel. There has since been an improvement in relations between Jordan and Israel, so at least trade has been resumed, the Israelis and Jordanians have been working together on projects in the lower Jordan River area, and production in the Jordan basin has seen major development. But has the problem of the refugees been solved? The **shacks and tent cities** on the border areas near Jericho and along the Jordan are now gone. But have the West Bank concerns been resolved? Hardly! **Jericho** is next door to Jordan, and even though it is much more peaceful than Gaza, much remains to be done.

3. **Syria lost** the **Golan Heights** and the productive farmlands almost up to Damascus. Some of the farmlands have been returned, but the Israelis are very hesitant about returning the **cliffs** of Golan to Syria, since Israel is not convinced that Syria will in fact recognize Israel's right to existence or that Syria will not use the heights as the base to launch future rockets on the cities and villages around the Sea of Galilee as they did in previous years. Having walked on the Golan Heights and been in the north during the war, it is not difficult to understand the Israeli hesitancy. All one has to do is look down on the plain below the heights, and the reason for doubt becomes clear. Has the problem been solved? Hardly! The situation remains a standoff.

4. Perhaps the **saddest aspect** of the story concerns **Lebanon**, which was not engaged in the earlier conflicts but has suffered the severest damage as a result of the conflict. Lebanon was perhaps the best example of a Middle Eastern country that had been able to integrate Muslims and Christians in government and business and it recognized the rights of many others, as well. Moreover, **Beirut was the jewel of the Middle East** and a delightful place to visit. But the massive influx of Palestinian refugees into Lebanon completely upset the conditions in the small peace-loving country. Failure to integrate the masses provided an intense seedbed for radicalism, which led to an incredible breakdown of understanding among the various groups in the population. **Syria**, seeing an opportunity to enhance its position in the Middle East, encouraged the festering of ill will so that it led to the Lebanese civil war that literally destroyed the city of Beirut. Moreover, the radical Palestinians used southern Lebanon as a launch-

ing place not only for firing rockets on northern Israel but also for terrorist attacks on schools and communities in that area. The result has been **Israel's counterattacks** on southern Lebanon, which could easily have reached Beirut if the early invasion had not been stopped by world pressure. The incursions into Israel have been reduced as the result of Israel's reactions, but has the problem of Lebanon been solved? Hardly!

5. It would not be fair to comment on the Palestinian Refugee Problem without a comment concerning **Israel** as well. The distinctions made in Israel between the **yellow license plates** for Israel proper and the **green license plates** for the Palestinian territories may be understandable, but it is merely a symbol of a much deeper problem that will take more than a wise Solomon or a tenacious Kissinger to solve. In past years, I usually traveled in vehicles bearing a yellow license plate, but I also have traveled in vehicles with green plates. The difference was incredible. Yellow plated cars were waived through checkpoints and proceeded on their way without hassle, whereas green plated cars were stopped, delayed, and often searched beyond reason for weapons or other matters. Now one cannot complain about the **importance of security**, and Israel is superb in matters of security. But the Jews who were forced to wear yellow identifying stars during the Nazi period should have learned that such treatment of singling out a particular group does not engender respect for authority or win over loyalty.

Accordingly, when I lived in the Middle East, it became very clear that with respect to any incident which arose in Israel, **Radio Tel Aviv** would report the matter one way and **Radio Amman** would report it differently. The **divide** is very great, and it only becomes greater with each incident. Will rockets solve the problem? Will bulldozing homes in response to attacks make life more secure? Will the building of the current wall keep terrorists out of Israel? Did having two types of education make for better understanding in Israel? Can hatred be overcome by bartering? Readers may answer, "Yes," "No," or, "Maybe," to those questions, but everyone should agree that the refugee problem is merely part of a much bigger concern that involves distrust, broken promises, and failure on the part of governments and people to be willing to live in harmony with each other and respect each other's differences.

One more issue needs to be addressed before leaving this matter. In 1917, the British, through Lord Balfour, issued **The Balfour Declaration** in which they promised the Jews a homeland, but they also promised not to infringe on the rights of the Palestinians. As a result, the influx of Jews from Europe increased beyond the earlier numbers that were arriving by small boats and other means—often under the cloak of darkness. The Arab Palestinians objected to the increasing numbers of immigrants and sought to control the situation during the 1930s. Then World War II and the Nazi holocaust occurred. After the war, the **United Nations** partitioned Palestine in an effort to satisfy **Israel's quest** for a homeland following the holocaust. But the question remains: Did they actually consider adequately the situation of **the Arab people** who were living in Palestine at the time? And did they provide sufficient incentives for peaceful living among both sets of inhabitants? It is one thing to **take a green pen in a meeting** of politicians and generals and draw a **border** on a map; it is quite another matter to deal authentically with people living in the land where the border is being drawn. The **Allies** may have **won the Second World War**, but it is exceedingly doubtful that they provided **peace in the Middle East!**

XI

VISITING JORDAN

J ORDAN IS OFTEN **VIEWED by readers of the Bible** as an attachment to the land of
Israel or Palestine in much the same way as the mountains of the Gilead, now known
as the Jordanian highlands; plus, Moab and Edom were viewed as an attachment to
the Kingdom of Israel in the time of David and Solomon. Indeed, **two and a half tribes**
(Reuben, Gad, and half of Manasseh) were allotted portions on the east side of the Jordan
River north of Moab when the people of Israel divided up the Promised Land.

THE LAND OF JORDAN

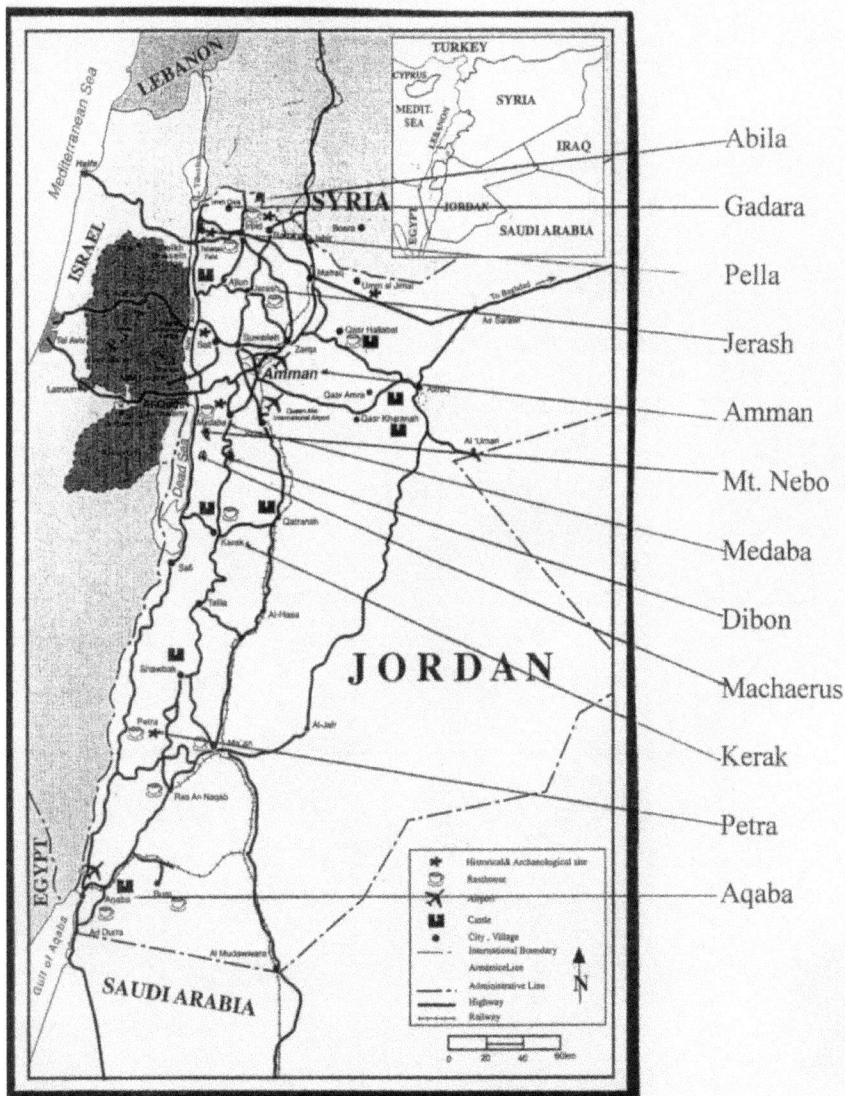

GENERAL INFORMATION ABOUT JORDAN

Today Jordan is a landlocked country, except for the southern port at Aqaba on the Gulf of Aqaba/Eilat. It is surrounded on the north by Syria and the Yarmuk River, at the end of the northeast corridor by Iraq, on the east and south by Saudi Arabia, and on the west by Israel along the Jordan River and the desert part of the Rift Valley. Currently, most people from the United States traveling to Jordan arrive either by plane at Queen Alia Airport in Amman or through one of the three primary border crossings from Israel: one near Beth Shan in the north, another at the Allenby Bridge near Jericho, or the third in the south at Ein Evrona near Eilat, which also provides access to the Sinai and thus Egypt by crossing a narrow strip of Israel.

Like Israel and Egypt, **one of the principle industries is tourism**. But besides entertaining visitors, its economy is supported by the textile, agricultural, and mining industries. The **currency** used is the **Jordanian Dinar**, which is equal to 1,000 fils.

The King's Highway and the Old Testament

Along the western edge of Jordan and through some of the highlands, runs the historic caravan road called the "King's Highway," or *al-Tariq al-Sultan* ("the Sultan's Highway), which was one of the major routes **connecting Mesopotamia to Egypt** and which armies used to attack, conquer, and subjugate Jordan. One can join the extension of this road at the **Euphrates River**, travel to **Palmyra and Damascus in Syria**, then move south into modern **Jordan** and pass by the magnificent city of **Gerasa** (or **Jerash;** one of the ten independent cities of the Decapolis in the time of Jesus). Continuing south, one comes to the **Jabbok River**, the same river where **Jacob** wrestled with the Lord and his name was changed to Israel (Gen 32:22–30). Then the road continues, passing near Jordan's capital city of **Amman,** named after Ben-ammi, the younger son of Lot by his second daughter and the ancestor of the Ammonites (Gen 19:30–38). Thereafter, the road passes through Moab near Mt. Nebo, where Moses gave his final addresses to the people of Israel (Num 32–36) and where on Mt. Nebo Moses was allowed to gaze at the Promised Land before he died (Deut 34:1–7). About five miles south, one now can come to the town of **Madaba** where the ancient mosaic map of the Holy Land was found. Then proceeding south into the desert for another twenty miles, one comes near to Dibon where the famous Mesha Stela (Moabite Stone) was discovered. South of the Dead Sea, **a branch road** at Bozrah leads through a pass to Kadesh Barnea and Via Maris near the Mediterranean Sea. But if one travels farther south on the highway, then it continues near the site where the ancient rose-colored fortress city of **Petra** lies hidden behind a narrow pass in the mountains about 180 miles south of Amman. Finally, the road reaches Jordan's south border at the **Gulf of Aqaba/Eilat.** The caravans that were headed for **Egypt** would then turn west and snake across the **Sinai** to their destination.

We turn briefly now to the early history of Israel and the King's Highway. Jacob left his uncle, Laban, and returned from Haran and the land of the Mesopotamia, and since he stopped at the Jabbok River in the hill country of the Gilead, he must have come along the King's Highway (Gen 31:17–21). Esau, who was the ancestor of the Edomites and the later Idumeans, must have come up from the south along this route to meet Jacob on his return and invited Jacob to join him (Gen 32:1–33:16). Instead of joining Esau in the southern part of the desert area or the Jordan Valley, however, Jacob turned west, crossed the Jordan River into Palestine, and headed south to Shechem (Gen 33:17–20) and on to Bethel (35:1–15); and during their southward trek, Rachael died in the vicinity of Bethlehem (35:16–21).

Later, Jacob sent Joseph to find his brothers, who had traveled north from home. He discovered they were grazing their sheep further north of Shechem close to Dothan— probably on the other side of the Carmel pass and in the pasture lands of the Galilee— perhaps near the Jordan River where the caravans that moved south would be traveling. The brothers seized Joseph and sold him as a slave to a group of Ishmaelite merchantmen headed for Egypt. These Ishmaelites were descendants of Abraham's son by the slave woman and lived in the desert, probably the ancestors of the Arabs. Did that caravan move west to the *Via Maris* and south through the Dothan Pass or east to the Jordan and the King's Highway, which would have been their familiar territory? That question is not settled. But the sale of Joseph served the brothers' purpose of getting rid of the pampered son of Jacob without killing him (Gen 37:12–28); thus began the story of the people of Israel in the land of Egypt.

A Brief History of Jordan

It is agreed by most scholars that the first inhabitants in area of the Jordan Valley may have appeared as early as 8000 B.C., but it was not until the third and second millennia B.C. (the Bronze Age) that settlements took root among the small groups of Ammonites, Moabites, Edomites, and Gileadites on the eastern side of the Jordan River. Small towns began to emerge about 2000 B.C., populated mainly by tribes from Arabia, the oldest of which the Bible calls the Horim, or Horites (from the Semitic word which means "dwellers in holes or caves"). These new settlers were probably seeking water for their flocks of sheep. Although there were periodic waves of marauders that robbed and devastated the villages, the towns generally enjoyed a fair sense of security from outsiders in this early period.

Beginning some time around 1750 B.C., howver, the situation began to change when the **Hyksos** (Shepherd Kings) from the north invaded the territory with their chariot forces as they were on their way to conquer Egypt. Warring tribes created confusion and unrest in the succeeding years. Sometime **after 1350 B.C.**, the **Israelites** moved through the land from the south after their release from slavery in Egypt. Two and one-half of their tribes settled in the country north of Moab, invading the territories of the Ammonites and the Gileadites. During the **period of the Judges** and through the time of **King Saul**, the Israelite settlers constantly skirmished with the Gileadites in the north and the Ammonites and Moabites in the south. Then **David** and **Solomon** succeeded in subduing most of what today is Jordan, but after Solomon's reign and the kingdom was divided (ca. 930 B.C.), the various peoples gained their **independence** from the control of the fractured Jerusalem monarchy.

Like the land of Palestine, the area of Jordan has been a crossing place for armies between the ancient superpowers of Mesopotamia and Egypt. The **Assyrians** began their march south around 800 B.C. and held the region until they were replaced by the **Babylonians** and after them the **Persians**, just as occurred on the western side of the Jordan in Palestine.

After the conquest of the entire area by **Alexander**, Jordan came under the control of the **Ptolemies of Egypt**, who held the territory until about 320 B.C. when the **Seleucids** grew more powerful, and shortly thereafter **Antiochus III** (the Great) conquered both Palestine and Jordan, wrenching them from Egypt. Thereafter, the entire area yielded to

Roman control in 63 B.C., but **nine major cities** on the eastern side of the Jordan River and the Sea of Galilee—**plus Beth Shan** on the western side of the Jordan River—were given a semblance of independence by Rome and designated as the **Decapolis** (ten cities). The rest of the area, especially during the Herodian period, was regarded as Perea and attached to the Galilee.

South of this region of Perea in the territory of **Edom**, an Arab people built a strong desert society known as the **Nabateans** with their capital at Petra. They were exceedingly shrewd traders and controlled the caravan route from Damascus through the desert. They possessed their own language, a form of Aramaic that gave birth to **Kufic** and ultimately to **Arabic.** So impressed was Mark Antony by the strength of the Nabateans and their culture that he gave as a special deed the lands around Petra to Cleopatra in order to satisfy her thirst for territory and wealth. But it was not really until about A.D. 106 that the Romans under Trajan actually succeeded in breaking the power of the Nabatean kingdom and incorporating it as part of their Roman provincial system. By 108 they were able to mint coins with the inscription, *Arabia aquisita* (not *capta*), indicating their optimism that the situation was under control.

As far as the contemporary Jordanians are concerned, the most important period for them was initiated in the seventh century with the rise of Islam in Arabia. They often cite the fact that in less than a century the Arab world had become dominant from Spain to the borders of China. Then beginning in 1099, indicative of the impact of the Crusaders in this area, along the western side of Syria and Jordan a number of Crusader fortresses began dotting the landscape. The remnants of that period stretch all the way from "Nimrod's Castle" (perhaps named after the supposed founder of Nineveh) near Mt. Hermon in what prior to 1967 had been Syria, all the way south through the Jordanian highlands.

In 1517, Jordan was invaded by the powerful Ottoman Turks, who remained in the country for four centuries before the British assisted the Arabs (led by Sherif Hussein of Mecca, the great-grandfather of King Hussein) in their 1916–1918 revolution against the Ottomans. Even though the Arabs hoped for independence, the British actually retained authority in Jordan. Then, in 1923 the British formally recognized the territory as an independent Emirate in Transjordan, but they actually maintained a mandate for controlling both Jordan and Palestine beyond that time. Finally in 1946, Jordan gained its independence and became the sovereign Hashemite Kingdom of Jordan with Emir Abdullah as the king.

APPROACHING THE VARIOUS SITES IN JORDAN

Travel in Jordan is done primarily by bus or automobile. Attention will be given to the principle sites in Jordan.

The City of Amman

Amman, the **capital** of Jordan, is a modern major desert city, having a population of over a million people. It is situated due east of Jericho and east of what has been known as the **Allenby Bridge** that crosses the Jordan River. The bridge, which replaced an earlier pontoon structure, was constructed in 1946 by the British before the end of the mandate and first Arab-Israeli War in 1948. It has since been **renamed** in honor of King Hussein. In contrast to its neighbor Jerusalem on the other side of the Jordan which has a gleaming golden hue in the sunlight because of the yellow tinged limestone with which the buildings are constructed, Amman has a brilliant white hue in the sun because of the white-colored stones and the marble used in its construction. Accordingly, it has often been called the "**White City**."

The biblical town of **Rabbath-Ammon** was the Ammonite capital as early as the time of the Exodus. Then during the Greco-Roman period, it was renamed **Philadelphia** and was regarded as one of the cities of the Decapolis. Like Rome it was originally built on seven hills, though today it is spread over more than twenty hills. Unfortunately, little remains from its rich heritage except the **Roman theater** complex, which seated about 6,000 people, located in the center of the modern city. Originally it had a beautiful colonnaded entrance with a garden of which a few ruins remain. Typical of the ancient Greek cities, an odeum (a miniature theater for smaller events) was nearby as well as a temple dedicated to the nymphs along with a fountain. Nearby, on the ancient acropolis (**Citadel**) are the ruins of the Temple to Hercules, which archaeologists indicate was built over the ruins of earlier temples or shrines. Most of the ancient buildings from this and other periods have served as construction resources for secondary use of the stones in later building projects. But evidences of the city walls can be found in several places, dating back from the Roman through the early Muslim periods. Outside the city, one can visit the remains of an impressive **Hellenistic Villa** that was uncovered by archaeologists.

The current visitor to **Amman** will discover that the city has grown rapidly over the past couple of decades and has had some difficulty keeping up with all the necessary improvement details. For instance, even though most of the amenities of a major city are available in Amman, the first-time visitor may encounter a little difficulty finding his or her way around the city because of the lack of street signs; however, help is available from hotels, taxi services, and other businesses.

One of the impressive sites in Amman is the **King Abdullah Mosque** with its large dome and twin minaret towers. Several smaller museums may be visited in Amman, such as the ones dedicated to historical and archaeological remains and to Jordanian costumes and jewelry, but none are as significant as the Israel Museum in Jerusalem or the Egyptian Museum in Cairo.

THE NORTH IN JORDAN

In the time of Jesus there was a group of cities mostly in Jordan that were designated as the Decapolis.

The Cities of the Decapolis in the Roman Province of Syria

The Decapolis was a group of ten cities in this area that Pompey recognized as significant and which Rome regarded as particularly oriented to Hellenistic culture and especially loyal to Rome. They were located in the midst of the otherwise hostile or contentious region of Syria (cf. Luke 2:2), over which an Imperial Legate chosen by the Emperor was given almost complete authority. The legate, or general, had at least one legion of troops to assist him in keeping order. This difficult region included such sub-areas as Judea, Galilee, Ituraea, Trachonitis and Abilene (Luke 3:1), and the legate would normally have local leaders such as tetrarchs and ethnarchs to assist him in keeping order, but in some situations the legate had middle supervisors like procurators/praefects, which were also appointed by the Emperor. During the period of the Herodian rulers, these Decapolis cities were viewed basically as cooperating partners but not usually as part of their domains.[1]

---

1. See my remarks on Gadara below.

Archaeologists have been able to recover the ruins of some of these cities, whereas others continue to be inhabited and contain a few remaining ruins, but some of the cities have all but ceased to exist. The following were the ten cities of the Decapolis:

— **Hippos** (for "horse"), on the eastern side of the Sea of Galilee; now in Israel, it is not mentioned in the Bible; although it has been surveyed, not much attention has been given to it.

— **Scythopolis** (Beth Shan), the only city on the western side of the Jordan River; it lies in Israel and attention to the magnificent ruins has been given in the section on "Lower Galilee" above.

— **Gadara, Abila, Pella,** and **Jerash** in the north of Jordan are treated in this section.

— **Philadelphia** (modern Amman) in central Jordan; it has been continuously inhabited and was discussed immediately above.

— **Damascus** in Syria; it will be reviewed briefly at a later point.

— Of less importance for our purposes are **Dion** (Dium, east of Abila) and **Kenath** (Canatha, which is mentioned in Num 32:42 and 1 Chr 2:23 and is the farthest east of the ten cities).

The City of Gadara and a Test Case for Biblical Interpretation: The Problem of the Demoniac in the Tombs

The story of Jesus healing the demoniac who lived in the tombs (Mark 5:1–20; Matt 8:28–34; and Luke 8:26–39) has caused scholars a little problem, and it obviously created a concern for **early scribes** as they transmitted the story to us. The reason concerns the name that was assigned to the people of the town where the story took place. The place is clearly on the eastern side of the Sea of Galilee. But the people in the story are **designated in three different ways** in our biblical manuscripts: in some of our manuscripts they are called Gadarenes; in other texts, Gerasenes; and in still others, Gergesenes. So here are the options:

(1) If the people had been **Gerasenes**, that would mean we are talking about Gerasa (or Jerash), a city in the Decapolis that we will treat shortly. But it is **thirty-seven miles** south of the Sea of Galilee and therefore rather unlikely.

(2) If the people were **Gadarenes** (another city of the Decapolis now known as Umm Qais or Um Qeis), which is certainly closer to the Sea of Galilee than Geasa/Jerash but presently is still nearly five miles south of the lake and indeed also on the south side of the Yarmuk River, since on the weight of our **best biblical manuscripts** Gadara is to be favored. Moreover, we have found ancient **coins** with the name Gadara inscribed upon them, along with a picture of a ship. Did the Sea of Galilee reach Gadara in the time of Jesus? The answer might be: Yes!

(3) But what about the **traditional site at Kursi** (on the present eastern shore of the Sea of Galilee), which has a fifth century Byzantine Church there and which commemorates the story of the dying pigs and the healing? Moreover, the cliffs of the Golan at that point could be the kind from which the pigs might have fallen into the Sea of Galilee if it was slightly enlarged.

The last option seems to be such a logical place, and that is the reason it was obviously chosen by the later Christians as the site. Moreover, the name Kursi could perhaps by a stretch be related to Gergesa. Yet we know very little about a group of people called the Gergesenes, and the best manuscripts would argue for Gadara instead of the traditional site. So which site would you choose? Does this example help you a little to understand better the kind of information that scholars weigh in making their decisions concerning the legitimacy of traditional sites?

The site of Gadara (Umm Qais) provides a splendid panoramic view of the surrounding countryside. From here it is possible to view Mt. Hermon and the Golan Heights in the north; the Sea of Galilee, Tiberias, and Mt. Tabor in the west; and the Jordan Valley to the south. After Antiochus III defeated the Egyptians in 218 B.C., the site was considered strategic, and a city was built here. Alexander Jannaeus seized the territory from the Seleucids, and Pompey wrested it from the Jews in 63 B.C. But it continued to be rather disconnected from Rome, and even though it was given to Herod the Great in 31 B.C. as part of his kingdom, it remained more attached to the Nabateans in the south. Vespasian destroyed the city during his tenure as the Imperial Legate in the Province of

Syria, though it survived as a weak center during the Byzantine period and declined during the Arab period. Most of the Hellenistic city lies in ruins today, although visitors can see the remains of what once were theaters and other buildings. The black basalt of the region that provided the building materials here offers a stark contrast to buildings in other cities. The large Governor's House from the Ottoman period has been restored as a museum and is open to the public.

The City of Abila

Northeast of Gadara on the ridge overlooking the Yarmuk River is Abila, a site that has been inhabited since the Bronze Age (for approximately 5,000 years). It served as the important district center for the eastern area during the Roman and Byzantine periods, but after the Arab conquest it declined precipitously and is basically abandoned today. The visible ruins of the city are not very significant.

The City of Pella

South of Beth Shan on the eastern side of the Jordan River near the northern Jordanian border lies the Decapolis city of Pella, which was named after the birth place of Alexander the Great in Macedonia. The place is not mentioned in the Bible and is now known as Tabaqat Fahl. It has today a few scattered remains at the site, but it is a place which must be mentioned here because of its historical significance.

Situated on the edge of what was once apparently a small lake in the Jordan River, the town was settled as early as the end of the Neolithic age (5000–4000 B.C.) and served as a Canaanite center. However, it fell into disuse during later periods and was not resettled until about the beginning of second century B.C. It became a significant city during the time of the Seleucids under Antiochus III, who captured the region from Egypt, but the Jewish Hasmonean King, Alexander Jannaeus, destroyed it in 83 B.C. because it was committed to Greek ways and refused to adopt Jewish rituals and patterns of life. It was rebuilt and became prosperous, having all the amenities of a Hellenistic city, before the end of that century following the coming of Pompey and the Romans in 63 B.C.

Its importance for our purposes here is that early Christians took very seriously the predictions of Jesus concerning fleeing from Judea and Jerusalem to the mountain areas when they saw the coming of the desecrating sacrilege, or armies surrounding Jerusalem (Mark 13:14–16; Luke 21:20–22). As a result, Pella became a city of refuge for Christians who fled Jerusalem during times of hostility and especially during the period of the Fall of Jerusalem (A.D. 66–70) and the Bar-Kokhba revolt of the Jews against the Romans in the time of Hadrian (A.D. 132–133). By the fourth century, the city had a Christian cathedral, a number of churches, and a monastery. But as the Arab forces swept over the land in A.D. 636, the city suffered severe devastation and decline. Finally, an earthquake destroyed the city and it never recovered.

The City of Jerash (Jarash or Garasa)

Popularly known as the Pompeii of the east, Jerash (originally named Garshu from which is derived the Greek name Garasa) is one of the best-preserved cities of the Decapolis. Located about twenty-five miles north of Amman and twenty miles east of the Jordan River, the colonnaded forum area of Jerash is simply magnificent to behold. The South Theater is equally well-preserved, as is the great triple arch of Hadrian constructed in A.D. 129 to honor his arrival in the city.

The site, according to archaeologist Nelson Gleuck, was probably first inhabited in the early Bronze period, and a few remains from the second millennium B.C. have been found; but the importance of the city began in the early second century B.C., after Antiochus III (Great) defeated the Egyptian Ptolemy and began constructing a Greek style city, which included an early Temple of Zeus built about 163 B.C. Similar to Pella, Josephus indicates that the Hasmonean Alexander Jannaeus captured the city for the Jews and attempted to force its citizens to adopt Jewish ways (*Ant.* xiii.393ff.). Then Pompey added the city to Roman authority in 63 B.C. During the first Jewish Revolt, the city was apparently captured briefly by the Jews but then recaptured by Vespasian before he left Palestine to assume the Imperial throne, and it did not suffer such a fate during the second Jewish Revolt. It gained in importance when the Romans subdued the Nabateans in A.D. 106, and it became part of the Roman Province of Arabia thereafter. A number of churches were built during and following the fourth century in the early Byzantine period,

31. The grand entrance to Jerash in Jordan

and an unconfirmed early Christian tradition has suggested that Paul spent his three years in "Arabia" (Gal 1:17–18) here at Jerash. Besides the large double chapel Cathedral with its mosaics and an inscription that can be dated to A.D. 400, among the remains of other churches, three (St. John the Baptist, St. George, and SS. Cosmas and Damian) are worthy of note, as they were built side-by-side during the first third of the sixth century before the Arab conquest in the seventh century.

In approaching the ancient site after passing the Arch of Hadrian, one comes to the large hippodrome, then to the great wall that encircled the city with its scores of towers. Inside the southern gate immediately on the left are the later Temple of Zeus and the South Theater with seating for about six thousand. In front, one sees the magnificent Colonnaded Forum in the shape of an ellipse, which leads directly into the Cardo (main street of the city) with many of its great columns standing and with two tetrapylons (squares). Among the remains of other buildings evident are several baths, a Nymphaeum (fountain to the nymphs), a smaller north theater and the Temple complex dedicated to Artemis with what must have been a majestic propylaeum (entrance) as well as the churches mentioned above.

THE SOUTH IN JORDAN

South of Amman, there are several sites that should be included in a visit to Jordan. While many more could be mentioned, of particular significance are Mt. Nebo, Medaba, Dibon, and Petra.

A Visit to Mt. Nebo (Mt. Pisgah)

While it is impossible to say for sure that the site designated as Mt. Nebo (Mt. Pisgah) is the biblical site, visitors to Jordan will want to stand on what tradition has assumed to be Mt. Nebo and glance over the landscape that **Moses probably saw before he died** (Deut 34:1–6). Situated about fifteen miles south west of Amman, five miles from Madeba, and about twelve miles due east of the northern edge of the Dead Sea where the Jordan River ends, the mountain rises to an elevation of 2,740 feet and has two peaks, Siyagha and el-Mukhayyat.

If one rises early in the morning—as I have done—and watches the sunrise while on the peak of **Siyagha**, the experience is truly one to remember. On a clear day you can **see far up the Jordan Valley** to the north; glimpse through the haze to **Mt. Gerazim** and the region of Samaria (modern Nabulus); view the heights of the **Mount of Olives** and thus Jerusalem; gaze upon the **Valley of Jericho**, Qumran, and beyond to the Herodian and **Bethlehem** in the background; and look south to **Ein-Gedi and Massada**. To help you in your viewing, a set of directional pointers is provided on the peak as one finds when one overlooks the valley from Mt. Carmel. Here, the **famed pilgrim Egeria** ascended the mountain in the latter part of the fourth century, and she witnessed what you can do by traversing the climb in a motor car or a bus. In her time, a monastery was already built here, but in the ensuing years of Muslim occupation it suffered badly. The church, which is dedicated to the memory of Moses on the peak, had been in ruins and was abandoned; recently, however, a **new chapel** has been erected for the benefit of pilgrims who visit the mountain.

At the base of the other peak (el-Mukhayyat), one finds the **Springs of Moses (Ayun Musa)**, which some traditions associate with the experiences at Kadesh (Num 20:2–9) and Horeb (Exod 17:6–7). Nearby, like on Siyagha, there were once thriving monastic settlements as there were on Mt. Sinai.

The City of Madeba (Madaba)

Madeba, which was a main stopping place on the ancient King's Highway for caravans, lies about twenty miles south of Amman. When the Israelites were making their way north on the east side of the Dead Sea to Jericho and the Promised Land, they were refused passage through the territory of Sihon, the King of the Amorites, leading Israel to conquer the entire area and to the burning destruction of Madeba (Num. 21:21–31). Later the Ammonite king, Hanun, assembled a huge army at Madeba (1 Chron. 19:7) with chariots from various states—including Syria—and forces from Mesopotamia to attack David and Israel, but the battle went in favor of Israel. As Isaiah looked to the future, he issued judgment on Moab that included Madeba and nearby Mt. Nebo (Isa. 15:2).

Today, the visitor to Madeba will still be able to see a portion of the old remains of Roman buildings and part of the old road, but something more important is located in the town. During the Byzantine period (from the fourth century for about four hundred years), Madeba attracted highly skilled artists, and it became the center for some of the finest mosaics in the entire south eastern Mediterranean region. Among the most renowned results of their work is the **Madeba Map**, which was brought to light in the final decades of the nineteenth century. It is a fascinating **mosaic** map that originally **measured eighty-one-by-sixteen feet**, showing the land of Palestine with the surrounding countries as they were known at the time. The sites are identified by Greek words and Jerusalem is at the center. The map is a pictorial representation of the sites and includes a basic plan of Jerusalem. It originally contained **more than 2,000,000 multicolored cubed stones** (in white, black, yellow, grey, red, blue, green, violet, and brown) and can be dated fairly precisely at A.D. 560–565. At the close of the nineteenth century, the Greek Orthodox Patriarch of Jerusalem ordered that a new church be built to house the map; unfortunately, during the building of the church, much of the map was destroyed by unskilled workers who simply ripped it up and were unable to reassemble it. Despite the tragic results, the extant remains of the map depict not only sites but also flora and fauna of the region during that time; therefore, the site is very much worth a visit.

Besides the map, there are several other places where fine mosaics can be seen. The mosaics of the **ancient church** are worthy of mention here, as is the **baptistery**. The **earliest** baptistery was below ground level, indicating that it was used for immersion, whereas a **later** baptistery was above ground, indicating that it was used for infusion (baptism by pouring). Other early mosaics can be found in the Churches of St. Elias (Elijah, ca. A.D. 600 with birds and animals), and of the Apostles (ca. A.D. 580 with a woman rising out of the sea).

The City of Dibon (Dhiban)

About forty miles south of Amman, twenty miles south of Madeba, and twelve miles east of the Dead Sea lies the city of Dibon, which was the earlier capital of Moab. The city was under the rule of Sihon, the King of the Amorites, before the Israelites destroyed the cities in the area and took possession of them as they journeyed to the Promised Land (Num 21:30). After the Israelite conquest, the tribe of Gad rebuilt the city (Num 32:34). Later, David conquered all of Moab and made it subject to his authority (2 Sam 8:2). During the period of the Divided Kingdom, **Mesha, the King of Moab,** had been paying heavy taxes to Ahab (the son of Omri), but when Ahab died, Mesha **rebelled against Jehoram** (the son of Ahab), so Jehoram sought the help of Jehoshaphat of Judah to regain his interests (2 Kgs 3:1–27).

Here at Dibon one of the great **archaeological treasures,** the **Mesha Stela (Moabite Stone)**, was discovered in 1868, confirming the rebellion of Mesha, the King of Moab (who claimed to be the son of Chemosh, the god of the Moabites), against the descendant of Omri. Although much of the stele was badly damaged later in an effort to sell pieces to competing parties, an impression had been made, allowing a reconstruction of a copy of the stele, which is now in the British Museum. The message on the stele not only confirms the rebellion of Mesha but also indicates that Mesha conquered a number of the cities of Gad, slew all the people at **Nebo,** fortified and improved the water works of **Dibon,** and also rebuilt **Madeba.** But as is typical of such congratulatory records, it says nothing of his defeats.

The Cities of Machaerus and Kerak

South of Dibon are the two fortress cities of Machaerus and Kerak, which require brief comments.

Machaerus was probably first constructed in the early part of the first century B.C. by the Hasmonean King and High Priest, Alexander Jannaeus, as one of his desert fortresses built to protect his eastern territories. It was occupied by the Romans with the coming of Pompey in 63 B.C. and became the desert outpost of Herod the Great in 20 B.C. It passed to Herod Antipas as his southern outpost for Perea after the death of his father. Here, Josephus indicates, **John the Baptist** was imprisoned, and after the dance of Salome, the daughter of Herodias, John was beheaded (*Ant.* xviii.116ff; cf. Mark 6:14–28).

On the slope of mountain pass guarding the ancient highway is **Kerak**, the biblical city of Moab that had several spellings, such as Kir-hareseth (-hares), and was a fortified city conquered by Jehoram, mentioned in the battles with King Mesha and the discovery of the Mesha Stela (2 Kgs 3:25; see also Dibon above). In the poetical predictions concerning the judgment on Moab in Isaiah, it is simply called Kir at 15:1, but it is also known as Kir-hareseth [-hares] at 16:7 and 16:11 (cf. Jer 48:31, 36). Some scholars have suggested that calling the place Kir-Moab would suffice to avoid confusion. The French erected a Crusader fortress on the site in the twelfth century, and the last of the French commanders, Renaud de Chatillon, was captured in the battle at the Horn of Hattin and beheaded by Saladin. The **view** from the fortress is impressive.

The City of Petra

A visit to the **rose-colored, rock city of Petra** (meaning "rock") is a magnificent one and should beckon every traveler to Jordan. **Hidden behind a narrow passage** in the southern sandstone mountains of the country and situated just over 180 miles south of Amman, the ancient city controlled the southern section of the King's Highway and became wealthy by demanding a **toll** from the caravans that passed that way. Although there are some indications that the area may have been inhabited as early as 10,000 B.C., not much is known about the city before 312 B.C. when the Macedonians tried unsuccessfully to conquer it. Some have thought that Petra is to be identified with the biblical Sela[2] (which also means "rock") but the connection is not certain.

The desert people who controlled the area were known as the **Nabateans**, and their rulers often bore the name Aretas.[3] The rugged Nabateans from Petra actually were so powerful that they were able in the third century B.C. to invade most of today's Jordan and succeed in **capturing Damascus** as well. As I indicated earlier, **Mark Antony gave Cleopatra** the gift of Petra, but Roman Egypt hardly controlled it. The Romans finally subdued Petra and the area in A.D. 106 and made it part of the Province of Arabia. In 131, **Hadrian** later brought an end to its significance by **diverting the rich trade from the east** to a new westbound route through **Palmyra**, which is north and east of Damascus; however, it regained some stature in the fourth century A.D. when the Romans divided the Province of Arabia and established Petra as the southern capital. Thereafter, it gradually **declined** to a small community of Christian monks in the Byzantine era and ceased to be significant during the Arab and later Muslim periods. The French Crusaders occupied the area for a brief time in the twelfth century, but today it lies **unoccupied**, except for those who are engaged in the tourist business.

The "hidden city" is a fascinating place with virtually no ancient abandoned residences to be seen at this time, although a few bedouin families have made their camps here. Archaeological work, however, continues in the inner areas of the huge complex.

After entering the area through a narrow passageway with massive rock walls on either side, the first-time visitor makes a sharp turn and is surprised to confront a huge carved façade in the rock wall with several entrances to a great carved cave that has commonly been called the "treasury" (**Khazneh**) because the Bedouins supposed that it contained riches hidden from the wealth of the past. Singing in the cave can be an interesting experience if one is with a group of people. As one proceeds further through the wadi, the site opens into a series of small plains with rock walls surrounding the area. What becomes quickly evident is that the walls are honeycombed with caves that were used pri-

---

2. For references to Sela (Selah; the "rock") see Judg 1:36, Isa 16:1, and Jer 49:16. Note also that in 2 Kgs 14:7, Amaziah stormed Sela and after conquering it, he renamed it Joktheel.

3. For example: not only was the name of the first Nabatean ruler of whom we know named **Aretas** (2 Macc 5:8), but the first wife of Herod Antipas was the daughter of a later Nabatean ruler by the same name who created conflicts for him by making thrusts into Herod's southern region of Perea after Herod divorced the daughter and married Herodias, who previously had been the former wife of Herod's half-brother Philip—who in turn was the father of Salome, who danced before Herod and demanded the head of John the Baptist (Mark 6:17–28). As you can see, seeking to understand the Herodians and the Nabatean rulers is an interesting exercise, and Herod the Great gave all of his sons the first name of Herod.

marily for **burial chambers**, some having interesting façades carved into the rock walls. Much of the site appears to be a **necropolis** (city of the dead).

As one continues, one reaches a **great theater** with a seating capacity for about 8,000 people (!), but it evidently has reused an area that was previously employed for tombs. Above the area is a ritual center with an **altar for sacrifice**. Beyond the theater, one comes to several more large tombs, including one to Sextus Florentinus. Further on, one enters **a large public area** containing a nymphaeum (fountain to the nymphs) and a colonnaded street that ends with a monumental gate. In this area are the remains of markets, several bathhouses, a palace, gymnasia, and a couple of temples—one to the god Dashara and another with winged lions to his partner, both of which the Bedouins attribute to the Pharaohs of Egypt, but they are Roman, probably from the second or third centuries A.D.

There are also remains of **Christian occupation** in the upper wadis, including a church and an impressive monastery, the façade of which resembles the "treasury" and which probably was originally carved in the third century and adapted by the monks for their use.

> **ADVICE TO VISITORS:** The complex of Petra is **extensive** and requires a good deal of walking (three to four hours) to see the entire area. Buses and cars are not allowed into the site. There are several **options** open to visitors. If one is traveling with a group and may be given a limited time for the visit, one may wish to engage a motorized cart to see the site. Or one can limit the visit to the front portion of Petra and walk through the entrance to the "treasury" and into the first section of the tombs and then return. This arrangement will provide an excellent taste of the site, although one will not see the distant part containing the public section of the city. Some visitors may enjoy engaging a donkey and keeper just beyond where the buses are parked, ride a donkey to the "treasury," then return by foot or donkey.

The Port of Aqaba

The southern terminus of the road in Jordan is **Aqaba**, which parallels Israel's port city of **Eilat** on the gulf. It has served as a major stopping point for **Muslim pilgrims** from North Africa, Palestine, Syria, and Jordan on their way to Mecca. Early Arab writers knew it as Ayla, and it also served as the port for early travels and trade to the Orient.

French Crusaders captured it in the early twelfth century and built a fortress here that was recaptured by Saladin in 1170. The current **Hashemites** gained control of it from the Ottomans in 1917.[4]

Please see my earlier comments in the sections related to travel in Israel and Egypt.

I will **NOT** here repeat the statements on security. Jordanian Security Forces will monitor your movements, so you should feel very safe.

I have already noted in the General information that the currency used in Jordan is the Dinar and that one Dinar is the equivalent of 1,000 fils.

However, I cannot reemphasize too strongly the serious **WARNING** I gave in the last chapter related to Egypt about **peeling all fresh vegetables and fruits. Failure to observe this warning can have serious implications for your health.**

Moreover, drink only bottled water, whether it is sparkling or still. Normal tap water in the hotels has **NOT been purified** sufficiently for the human system. This warning also applies to **brushing your teeth.**

---

4. For further information concerning the Gulf of Aqaba/Eilat see Eilat above.

XII

NOTES ON VISITING SYRIA AND LEBANON

EVEN THOUGH NOT TOO many people who visit the Bible lands today also visit Syria and Lebanon (because of the unrest in those countries), it is important to provide the reader with a brief review of some of the sites in that region by someone who has been there.

THE LANDS OF SYRIA AND LEBANON

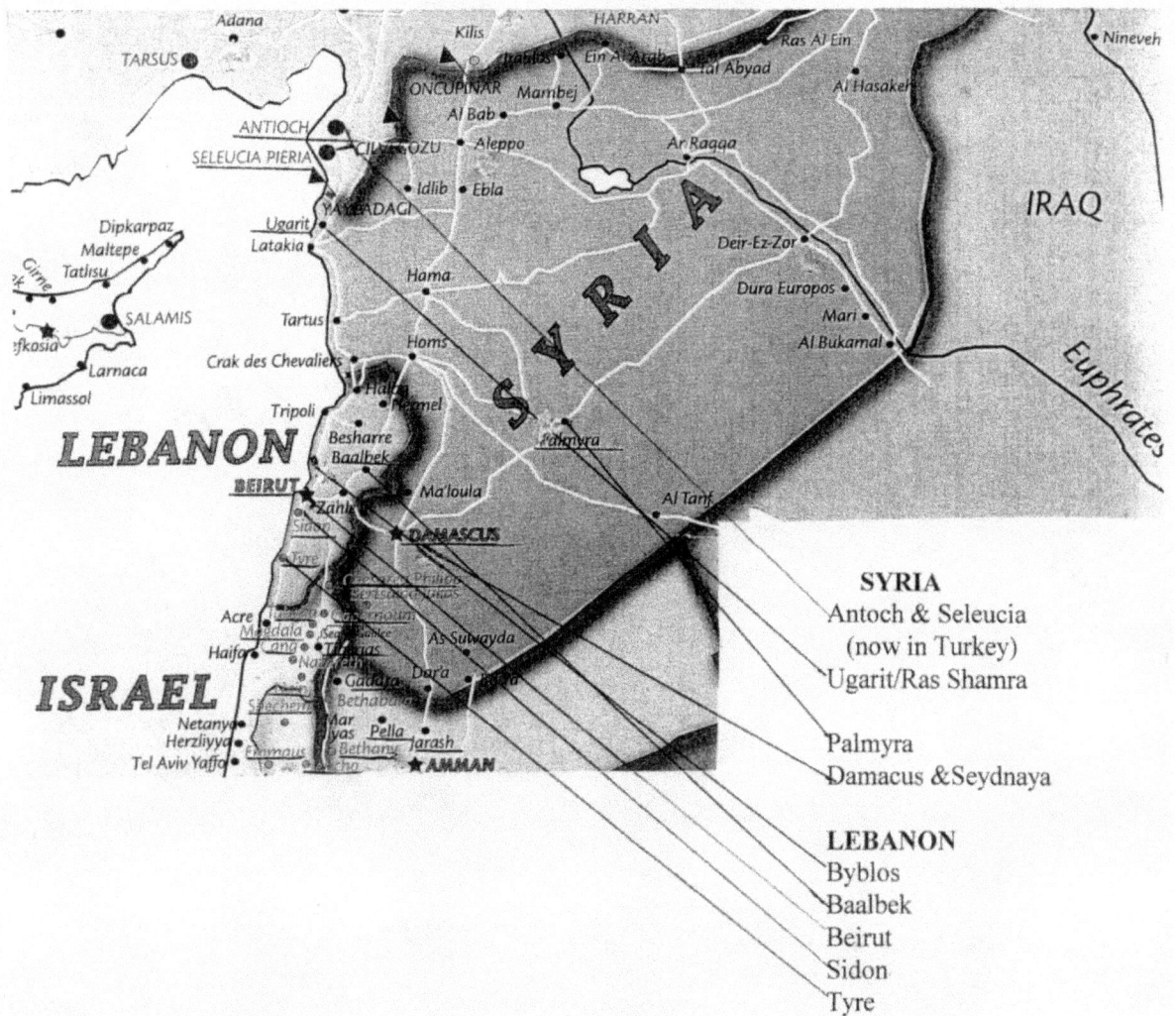

SYRIA
Antoch & Seleucia
(now in Turkey)
Ugarit/Ras Shamra

Palmyra
Damacus &Seydnaya

LEBANON
Byblos
Baalbek
Beirut
Sidon
Tyre

NOTES ON SYRIA

Syria is one of the oldest civilizations in the lands of the Fertile Crescent. Situated on ancient trade routes that joined merchants from the Far East with Africa and with Europe, Syria was an important player in the history of the early Israelites, as well as the people from the area of the Tigris and Euphrates lower basin and from Egypt and the Nile. A little later it played a role in relations between Greece and Rome. Today it is a major actor in the relations between the Arab states and Israel.

Syria (which is Greek for "high land") in Old Testament Hebrew was often called **Aram**, after the ancestor of the Arameans. But it is speculated that the Greek name Syria is derived from the name Tyre (Tzur), the city on the coast of modern Lebanon with whom the Greeks and Romans traded. Since the period of the Mandate (see below), it is bordered on the north by Turkey, on the east and south by Iraq, then further south by Jordan, and on the west by Palestine (Israel)—including the Sea of Galilee and the Golan Heights, then north of Israel by Lebanon, and finally further north by a small access to the Mediterranean Sea.

A Brief History

While there is evidence that people were settled in the area of Syria prior to the fourth millennium B.C., it was inhabited principally by Semites in the middle of the fourth millennium. Most of our knowledge concerning Syria begins in the middle of the third millennium with the ancient city of **Ebla** in northern Syria. The city and region around it, which **preceded the time of Abraham** by about five hundred years, may have had a population of about a quarter of a million people. It was a powerful, rich and a fairly advanced society that controlled less powerful city-states in the region. The language spoken was Semitic, similar to Hebrew, but the writing on many tablets that were found by archaeologists in their excavations of the city during the 1960s and '70s is in **cuneiform** (a form of writing that is still being researched).

Damascus and Aleppo (the two major cities of Syria today) became major centers on the caravan routes around 2000 B.C. The Amorites became a significant force in Syria about 300 years later, and the Arameans became the dominant force in Damascus about

200 years later, which correlates with much of the Old Testament period. The Assyrians conquered Syria around 732 B.C. just prior to the fall of Samaria and the Northern Kingdom of Israel in 722 B.C. The Babylonians also took Syria along with both Israel and Judah in the beginning of the sixth century B.C. They in turn were followed by the Persians in 538 B.C. and in 333 B.C. the Macedonians who were their conquerors. After Alexander died in Babylon, the Seleucids (headquartered in Antioch) constantly vied with the Ptolemies of Egypt for control of Palestine.[1] Then in 64 B.C., Pompey and the Romans gained control of Syria, and during the Byzantine period it became officially a Christian province.

The Muslim domination began with the conquest of the Arabs in A.D. 636. Damascus became the center of Muslim domination of the entire region under the Omayyads in 661, and the Abbasids from Baghdad overthrew them in 750. During the several centuries following the turn of the millennium, the Crusaders held the land for a short time, but Saladin and his successors from Egypt ousted them. The Mamelukes then kept control until the Ottomans from Turkey displaced them in 1516. Western influence became significant three hundred years later, and during World War I, Great Britain aided the Arabs in gaining their independence from the Turks. After the war, the entire region was divided into **four sections—Syria, Transjordan, Palestine, and Lebanon**—by the allies and the League of Nations. **France** was given a **mandate** over Syria that lasted until 1946 when Syria gained its independence and entered into conflict with Israel.

A Brief Biblical Review

Among the stories in the Old Testament that relate to Syria, the following should be mentioned. When Terah and his son Abram left the southern Mesopotamia basin and journeyed to Haran (Gen 11:31–32), they came into modern Syria. Then Jacob in fleeing from Esau came to his uncle Laban's home in Haran and gained his wives and concubines there (Gen 29–30). In the eleventh century B.C., Saul fought the Syrians, but it was David who conquered Hadadezer of Zobah in northern Syria along with the forces aligned against him from Damascus (1 Chr 18:3–8). Later Asa, the King of Judah, sought the help of Ben-hadad of Damascus to ward off the incursions of Basha, the King of Israel (1 Kgs 15:16–22). And still later, Ahab, the King of Israel, gained several defeats against

---

1. See the record in Daniel 11.

another Ben-hadad of Damascus, but since Ahab did not kill him as God instructed him, it meant that the Syrians would later return (1 Kgs 20:1–43).

Among the stories in the New Testament related to Syria is the account of the **pre-Christian Saul/Paul**, the envoy of the Jewish High Priest, who sought to stamp out early Christianity by capturing Christians; however, on his way to **Damascus** he was blinded by the risen Jesus, and after a visit from Ananias, Saul/Paul became a Christian proclaimer (Acts 9:1–22). Moreover, the early Seleucid and Roman capital of **Antioch** became a major force in the missionary expansion of Christianity, because here the "followers of the Way" were first **called "Christians"** (11:26). From Antioch, Paul and Barnabas set out for Cyprus on the first missionary journey recorded in Acts 13:1–3, and here the question concerning the necessity of Gentiles becoming Jews in order to become Christians was raised, leading to the Jerusalem Council recorded in Acts 14:24–15:35.

VISITING SOME OF THE SITES IN SYRIA

There are a number of sites that could be mentioned, but attention is directed inland to Damascus and Palmyra. On the Mediterranean coast are Ugarit and the ancient Syrian sites of Antioch, its harbor city of Seleucia, and its ancient recreational center of Daphne, which are now in modern Turkey.

Damascus

Damascus, the historic capital of Syria, is a fascinating place to visit. It is a major modern city of over 1,000,000 people, but residents there often make the claim that it is the oldest continuously inhabited city in the world. The city lies in a nearly arid plain, but through it flows the Barada River that has provided sustenance to the area for centuries.

Here, the blind Paul was brought to a place on a street called "Straight," which despite not being very straight (Acts 9:11) was an ancient way that ran from the western side to the eastern part of the ancient city. That part of the city today is very old and the streets are very narrow. While only a small part of the old Roman wall still survives, visitors may wish to pause in the chapel that is built into the **Keesan Gate**, where it is said that Paul was lowered in a basket in his flight from Damascus (Acts 9:23–25).

Among the other sites that should be visited are the beautiful **Omayyad Mosque** built in A.D. 705, which stands on the site of the earlier pagan temple to the **Aramean god, Hadad**, after which many of the early Syrian rulers were called "Ben-hadad" ("son of Hadad"). This temple gave way to the temple of the Roman god Jupiter and was later replaced by a Christian Basilica of John. Inside the mosque is a shrine to John the Baptist, and outside is a Minaret to Isa (Jesus). The mosque lies near the **Hamydieth Bazaar** (*souk el Hamydieh*), the major bazaar in the city. It is covered with a curved iron roof and is usually filled with people looking for bargains. South of the mosque is the twelfth century Mausoleum of Salah Edin (Saladin) who inspired art and architecture among Muslims.

Elsewhere in the city one finds the **El Azem Palace**, built by the governor of Damascus in 1750 with a hall for visitors (*salamelek*) and a beautiful one for women and children (*Haramelek*), housing fine representations of Damascian artistry. Also, worth photographing is the grand **Suleimanieh Mosque** (*al Takyeh al Suleimanieh*), with its double minarets. The visitor will also want to spend some time in the **National Museum of Damascus**, where one can see the restored façade of the Omayyad Palace of Kasr El Heir, the magnificent Tomb from Palmyra of Yarhai, as well as frescoes from the Dura-Europa Synagogue. Particularly of significance is the section dedicated to Syro-Oriental Antiquities, which contains the findings from the archaeological work done at **Mari** (3000–2000 B.C.) and at **Ras Shamra** (1400–1200 B.C.), two extremely important sites for anyone studying the ancient Middle East.

About **twenty-five miles** from Damascus is a **Christian convent** known as **Seydnaya**, which is inhabited by Greek Orthodox nuns. The convent is associated with a **legend** concerning **Emperor Justinian**, who in A.D. 541 was leading his forces against the Persians when he went looking for water. He came upon a deer that he decided to hunt. When he was ready to kill it with his bow, it turned into a woman whom he assumed was the Virgin Mary and who directed him to establish a convent there. Whereupon he instructed builders to comply with the Virgin's directions, and his sister is said to have become the first mother superior of the convent. An interesting twist is that the Syriac word *seydnaya* has two meanings: "our Lady" and "a site for hunting!"

Palmyra

Palmyra is known as "the **Bride of the Desert**," situated at about the midpoint for the ancient caravans who made their way between the great cities on the Euphrates and the Mediterranean Sea. It lies about **150 miles northeast of Damascus** and was built on the site of a major desert oasis.

It has had a long history associated with the ancient caravans, but it was made even more important when the **Romans** in the middle of the second century A.D. **directed the goods** from the east through Damascus **to the ports** on the Mediterranean and away from Egypt and the Kings Highway, thereby dealing an economic blow to the proud toll chargers of Petra who controlled that other caravan route. The Romans kept a force in Palmyra to protect the caravans, but in the middle of the second century when the garrison was depleted and the Persians attacked the city, **Odenathus, the Prince of Palmyra**, was able to repel the attackers, won for himself a commendation from Rome, and was elevated to the supreme commander of Rome in the east. When he died, his wife, **Zenobia**, assumed control and sought to extend her authority as far as Egypt, displacing Rome, which was promptly countered by the Roman legions. Palmyra was destroyed in A.D. 274. Since the city was exceedingly important, however, Diocletian ordered it rebuilt, and by the beginning of the third century it was again serving as the principal Roman outpost in the desert. The city was subsequently destroyed in the seventh century by the Muslims and has not since gained its former stature.

Nevertheless, the ruins of the Roman city provide a marvelous opportunity to examine structures from the past for those who are able to travel there. The principal "god" at Palmyra was the **Semitic Bel**, whose **temple** at Palmyra is in a remarkable state of existence and displays a fascinating **syncretic** mixture of eastern and western cultures in its Oriental-Roman construction, with its domed roof decorated by the images of the seven planets, the central sanctuary having two recesses for the altars with two bronze and golden gates, and the remains of what must have been a grand courtyard with a pool for ablutions by the priests. Also here are the early second century fertility Temple of Baal-Shameen, magnificent pillared walkways, a great arch, and a cemetery in a Valley of Tombs. There is also here a modern museum with desert art and the **Citadel** of Fakhreddin Ben Maan, which dates to the sixteenth century surrounded by a moat at the top of the nearby mountain. The view from the citadel is captivating.

Antioch on the Orontes (Antakya) and the Vicinity

The Roman capital of the large province of Syria (which included the sub-province of Palestine) was **Antioch**, where the official **Legate** of the Roman Emperor resided when he was not engaged in combat. Here, the Seleucids had earlier built their capital and near here they constructed a major seaport named **Seleucia** with a fortified passageway from the port to the capital. Nearby there was also built a recreational or "playboy" center named **Daphne**, which was like an ancient Las Vegas in which all types of partying took place on a regular basis. Indeed, *Daphnici mores* was a proverbial Latin phrase that indicated the lowest form of human morals. It would have been viewed somewhat like Corinth in the ancient world.

Antioch was the third largest city in the Roman Empire after Rome and Alexandria. By the end of the fourth century a.d., the population may have reached a half million by some estimates. In A.D. 540 the Persians, encouraged by the weakness of Rome, sacked the city and left it in a heap of ruins. The city never recovered from the blow by the Persians, and today it is a small, rather nondescript community named **Antakilyeh**.

As noted earlier, the followers of Jesus and "the Way" were first called "**Christians**" here. The question that one must ask is: Was that designation a **nickname**, and was it intended to be derogatory? Antiocheans were known for giving nicknames to people. **Antiochus IV**, who desecrated the Temple in Jerusalem, thought he was supreme even beyond his brilliant warrior ancestor of the same name. He proudly called himself Antiochus Epiphanes ("appearance of god"), but he angered even the citizens of Antioch who gave him the nickname "**Epimanes**" ("madman"). And later the Roman Emperor, Julian (the Apostate), who sought to picture himself like a philosopher with a long beard and failed to respect the Antiocheans and their practices, was called by them "**the goat.**" Moreover, because he sacrificed so many animals to the gods, they also called him "**the butcher.**" Nicknames can begin with derogatory intentions, but they can later become accepted as badges of significant meaning. Such was the case with such designations as "Protestant," "Baptist," and "Methodist."

Ancient Antioch was excavated by Princeton Universoity in the 1930s, and some points should be noted here. The city was dedicated to **Tyche**, the god of "Good Fortune," and his likeness appeared on the coins of the city. Moreover, a statue of the god had been carved and was set in the square of the city; like many such statues, it is now housed in the Vatican Museum. In addition, there was a tradition that during the time of Antiochus Epiphanes a **terrible plague** broke out, killing many citizens, and Leisus, their local necromancer, divined that the bust of **Charon**—the ferryman who transported people over the River Styx in the Underworld—should be carved in the cliff above the city. In addition, there were in the city many superb **mosaics**, including a beautiful woman goddess that is still on display there, and the even more impressive huge mosaic of the phoenix engulfed with roses, the ancient symbol of rebirth from the ashes, can be seen.

Also of note is the fact that workmen who were digging a well in 1910 came upon a silver cup that is now known as the **Chalice of Antioch**, which was purchased by the Metropolitan Museum of Art in New York. Measuring about seven and one-half inches tall and six inches in diameter at its widest point, it has an inner cup and an ornate outer cup which displays the figures of what are considered to be the early apostles around the central figure of Jesus. When it was first discovered, speculators argued that it was the so-called "Holy Grail" from the first century and contained the earliest, perhaps authentic, representation of Jesus in existence. Now that more study has been done and saner minds have prevailed, the cup is regarded to be from the Byzantine period. Some have suggested it may be from the late second century; however, it is probably older, and it contains an artist's rendition of Jesus.

In summary, ancient Antioch was a **great crossing point where east and west met** both in terms of trade and ideas. But it was also a place where the worst sorts of human morality were practiced. It was an excellent place for understanding the nature of humanity and therefore a significant site for the **launching of a missionary movement** that would provide God's positive alternative to the pagan religions, which were unable to provide adequate responses to the inner cries of the human psyche.

Ugarit (Ras Shamra)

On the shore of the Mediterranean Sea south of Antioch stands the ancient Tel Ras Shamra ("the Mound of Fennel"), which was discovered by accident in 1927. It has since been the subject of numerous archaeological campaigns and has furnished the world with important insights into the Canaanite civilization. The site is undoubtedly the famous city of Ugarit mentioned in the Amarna letters as a strategic center of Canaanite life in the second millennium B.C. It stood as a powerful force against Egyptian domination of the region and reached its zenith in the sixteenth century. It was destroyed around 1200 B.C., and the site was basically abandoned thereafter.

NOTES ON LEBANON

We come now to the final area of consideration for visitors to the Levant, or the lands of the Bible, which is the country of Lebanon. The current nation of Lebanon is the fourth region that the League of Nations carved out of the eastern Mediterranean section of the Fertile Crescent. The other sections that have already been discussed are Palestine (both Israel and the Palestinian Territories), Jordan, and Syria. This area has a rich history and encompasses some historic city-states that were significant Phoenician ports such as the early city of Byblos (which is north of the modern city of Beirut) and the later cities of Sidon (which is south of Beirut) and Tyre (which is south of Sidon and just north of the border with modern Israel).

Lebanon is a rather small nation stretching north to south about 120 miles and west to east about fifty miles. It is a very mountainous country, having a narrow costal plain facing the Mediterranean Sea that is generally less than five miles wide and in which Beruit and the historic ports are located. To the east of the coastal plain is a coastal mountain range known as the Lebanon Mountains, running from north to south. Then to the east of these mountains is a high plain or plateau now known as Al Biqa, through which the Litani River flows and exits into the Mediterranean through a pass in the mountains just north of Tyre. To the east of the plateau is another mountain range known as the Anti-Lebanon Mountains that are on the boarder with Syria. In the plateau (Al Biqa) and in the foothills of the Anti-Lebanon Mountains lies the famous religious complex known as Baalbek which I will discuss below.

A Brief History

The history of Lebanon—and particularly the City of **Byblos**—may have had its origin as early as 5000 B.C., but it was not until the early part of the third millennium B.C. that we are more aware of its trade in timber (the famous cedars) with Egypt. A seafaring people known as the Phoenicians, who were navigators and traders, settled the area. The name is likely derived from the Greek word *phoinix* ("reddish purple"), which in turn may have come from the name *Canaan* that means "land of purple" that undoubtedly arose from the fact that the region produces a brilliant purple dye regarded as extremely royal and valuable by the ancients. The name was applied to the strip of land along the eastern section of the Mediterranean Sea that involved not only Lebanon but also the lands of Palestine (Israel and the Palestinian Territories) and the western section of Syria. These Phoenicians were not only traders but also explorers, and they developed colonies throughout the Mediterranean basin as far west as Utica and Carthage in North Africa, Palermo in Sicily, and Sardinia and even Cadiz in southern Spain.

The pattern of conquests and invasions of Lebanon follows a similar one to most of the other lands of Bible through the Roman and Byzantine periods. The Arab invasion, however, avoided most of the Lebanese mountain areas, and Islam did not come into the region until the ninth century, resulting in Christianity being much stronger in Lebanon than in other parts of the region. In the eleventh century, the French Crusaders gained a strong foothold in Lebanon, and the Lebanese Christians were supportive of the French attempts to recapture the land of Palestine. In the sixteenth century, the Ottoman Turks invaded Lebanon and held the territory until the defeat of Turkey in the First World War. Following the war, the League of Nations gave France a mandate over the territory. After much jockeying for independence, the French finally left Lebanon in 1946.

With the Arab-Israeli War of 1948, Lebanon, which had not been a party to the war, was dealt a stinging blow by the influx of many thousands of Palestinian refugees who upset the peaceful balance that had been achieved between Muslims and Christians in the country, even though the Christian communities were generally more prosperous and actually had more power in the government than the Muslim communities. Since that time, the situation has been very unsettled in Lebanon, with a rebellion on the part of the Muslims in 1958. As a result of the war and the arrival of American troops, a settlement was reached that gave Christians and Muslims equal shares in the government.

But the presence of more than 350,000 unsettled refugees who made frequent guerilla attacks on Israel led to several retaliations by Israel. Then a civil war between Christians and Muslims broke out in 1975, literally devastating the country and ruining Beirut, which was the "Jewel of Middle East." This civil war was followed by a war between the Christians and Syrian troops in 1978 and 1979. And the Palestinian Liberation Organization (PLO) from the Palestinian territories continues to be active among the refugees. An adequate solution to this problem has not yet been forthcoming, even though the United Nations continues to be a buffer between the refugees and the Israelis. As Christians, it is our solemn duty to pray for peace in the Middle East and do all we can to assist in the resolution of the Palestinian problem.

A Brief Biblical Review

Lebanon is mentioned in the Bible as early as Deuteronomy 1:7, where Moses addressed the people and indicated that God directed the Israelites to **possess all the lands** to the Euphrates river, **including Lebanon.** Despite the fact that Moses longed to see Lebanon (Deut 3:25) and hoped that the people of Israel would possess its territory (Josh 1:4), his desire was not fulfilled; nevertheless, **Joshua did reach Mt. Hermon** (Josh 11:17), and Israeli territory now also includes a part of that mountain.

The "**cedars**" and the gardens of Lebanon are mentioned many times in the Bible as symbols of a pleasant and desirable land, and the Lebanese trees were regarded as valuable **building materials.** Indeed, Hiram, the King of Tyre (Lebanon), supplied building materials that included not merely cedar and cypress timber but building stones from the quarries of Lebanon for Solomon's construction of the **temple in Jerusalem** (1 Kgs 5:1–18). Hiram also sent cedar to **David** to build his palace (2 Sam 5:11 and 1 Chr 14:1), but in 2 Chronicles the king who sent the building materials to Solomon is called Huram (2 Chr 2:3–11). But please remember that I earlier indicated that vowels in **Semitic languages** are not consistent![2] Later, in the time of Zerubbabel, the people of both Sidon and Tyre again supplied the cedar timbers for the construction of the **second temple** (Ezra 3:7). Another interesting side note in Jeremiah 18:14 is a reminder that Lebanon receives a good deal of **snow**, and those who live in Israel today know that you can **ski on Mt. Hermon** in the winter.

---

2. See CHAPTER III, p. 14.

While Tyre and Sidon are often mentioned together in the Bible, Sidon is sometimes mentioned separately (e.g., Gen 10:15–19); however, Tyre is mentioned separately more times, particularly in the time of David and Solomon. Although Tyre and Israel were on good relations during that time, the relationship did not continue indefinitely, and the **prophets** later called down **destruction**—in a few cases promising restitution—on the area of Lebanon (Isa 23:1–18; Jer 25:22; Ezek 26–28; Amos 1:9–10; etc.).

In Roman times, the lands of Palestine—including Galilee, Iturea, and Lebanon—all belonged to the super Roman Province of Syria, and the borders were not as firm as they are today; nevertheless, the area was still distinct, as indicated by the statement concerning Herod Agrippa I who threatened to cut off grain and other supplies to Tyre and Sidon (Acts 12:20). **Jesus** actually went into the region of Tyre and Sidon and healed the **daughter of a Canaanite woman.** My students often have difficulty understanding the woman's exchange with Jesus when she uses the illustration concerning the "**dogs**" but it is important to remember that in an old Jewish prayer, religious Jewish men daily thanked God that they were not born Gentiles, slaves, or women. They often regarded Gentiles to be dogs! But Jesus did not agree to such a designation and healed Gentiles (Mark 7:24–31 and Matt 15:21–28; see also the healing of the Gentile in Gadara in Matt 8:28–34). Not only did Jesus go to Lebanon, but the people of Tyre and Sidon also came to hear him (Mark 3:7–8 and Luke 6:17), and he indicated that the Gentile cities of Tyre and Sidon would be regarded as better off in the coming judgment than the Jewish cities of Chorazin and Bethsaida that had witnessed many works of Jesus and refused to repent and accept him (Matt 11:20–22 and Luke 10:13–14). Paul stayed for about a week in Tyre on his third missionary journey before being imprisoned (Acts 21:3–4).

Visiting Some of the Sites in Lebanon

Although very few pilgrims visit Lebanon today because of the unrest in the area, mention must be made concerning some of the sites and particularly Baalbek, Tyre, Sidon, and Byblos.

Baalbek

I could wish that everyone who visits the lands of the Bible could also visit Baalbek. Taking about **300 years** to construct in the foothills of the Anti-Lebanon Mountains and situated just over fifty miles from Beirut (ancient Berytus), the remains of the temples at Baalbek provide an example of some of the **grandest** and **most picturesque building sites** in the world. Unfortunately, at present those temples lie very near one of the largest Palestinian refugee camps in the Bekaa Valley near the source of the Litani River.

The **Temple of Jupiter** at Baalbek provides an important perspective on Hellenistic thinking because this temple is not to be identified with the "Jupiter" of Rome. At Baalbek, Jupiter was viewed as a Semitic sun god and linked with the Canaanite understanding of Baal that encompassed the pantheon and was associated with fertility worship that was current throughout the Levant, the area stetching from the borders of the Sinai through Israel and north into Lebanon and Syria.

This temple must have been truly magnificent in its day because it was built on a constructed platform with huge underground vaults for the storage of grains and other items, as well as for the housing of animals. This Hellenistic temple was second only in size to the great temple of the Olympian Jupiter in Athens and measured 310 feet in

32. The remaining six magnificent pillars of the Grand Temple of Jupiter at Baalbek (Note the tiny size of humans in the picture)

length and 175 feet in width, but it far surpassed in grandeur that Athenian Jupiter because of its location. It was larger than the earlier Parthenon dedicated to Athena from Hellenic times but must have compared favorably in grandeur with its glistening rival on the Acropolis in Athens.

The **foundation stones** of the temple of Jupiter each probably weigh about **800 tons** and were of the trilithon design (three huge stones joined together as a base) and so well-engineered that you could not put a razor blade between them. Each stone measured sixty-four-by-fourteen-by-twelve feet, and they may have been some of the largest stones ever used in the construction of a building. The **six gigantic pillars** that were still standing when I last visited the site—in spite of the violence in the area—rise to a height of more than sixty-five feet and are more than seven feet in diameter at the base, dwarfing most

anything around it. Moreover, these huge pillars of the Temple of Jupiter were constructed without cement, and the three sections of each of the pillars were joined with a small iron dowel and set up by means of precise mathematical centering in connecting the stones. They are topped with grand Corinthian capitals.

Nearby is the smaller, yet magnificent **Temple of Bacchus**, much of which is still standing, including twenty-five of its original forty-six columns. The huge doorway to the temple provides an excellent example of superb Hellenistic construction with two large stones for the lintel and a great keystone—one of the largest I have seen—that held the doorway in place. Within would have stood the figure of the god, and in the darkened front of the temple

33. The Great Temple of Bacchus at Baalbek with one of the best classic keystones still in existence

(the cella) the sexual nature rituals that allegedly promoted fine harvests and the expansion of one's livestock would have taken place in the dark recesses of the temple. The temple walls were graced with beautiful ornamentation, some of which can still be seen.

The courtyards and surroundings must have also been magnificent. Nearby, one can see an even larger stone block that was not used but may have either been rejected or been intended for some future use. But it serves as an indication that the ancients were able to chisel and move incredible stones in their construction projects. It measures seventy-by-sixteen-by-fourteen feet and easily must weigh 1,500 tons. Where it would have been used is still a mystery.

A visit to this sight, like a visit to the pyramids of Egypt, provides contemporary people with insights into the amazing building and engineering skills of the ancients. It is hoped that the unrest in Lebanon will soon end, and visitors will be able to return to see this magnificent temple complex.

Tyre

Along the Mediterranean coast and just over ten miles north of the border with Israel lies the historic Phoenician city of Tyre, which today is the center for many Palestinian refugees but in the ancient world was one of major trading cities. From Tyre, goods were shipped from Mesopotamia and Arabia to all parts of the Mediterranean basin and as indicated above Tyre established colonies as far away as Carthage and Utica in North Africa.

Tyre was very prosperous, and its purple dye and glassware were well-known. Its prosperity and independence from Egypt began just prior to the time of David and continued until the coming of the Assyrians and Babylonians—even then it retained a sense of isolation because most of the city was built on an island just off the Mediterranean coast. The Tyrians were a proud, independent people and resisted Babylonian domination, but after more than ten years of resistance, Nebuchadnezzar II finally had enough of their rebellion and in 573 B.C. brought Tyre under subjection. Indeed, later the Tyrians proudly challenged Alexander to conquer them when Byblos, Berytus (ancient Beirut), and Sidon handed over their fleets to the great general as he was marching south from Asia Minor to take the entire region as far south and west as Egypt. Alexander accepted the challenge and built a causeway from the mainland out to the island, and after seven months he sacked the city in 322 B.C. This resulted in the town of Tyre being connected to the mainland. The Romans later controlled the city, and it became part of the Eastern Byzantine empire after Constantine. During the Crusades, the Europeans made Tyre one of their principal fortress cities, until it fell to the Muslims in 1291.

As indicated above, Hiram, the King of Tyre, was on friendly relations with David and supplied him with masons and carpenters to build his palace (2 Sam 5:11), and the Tyrians supplied Solomon with building materials for the construction of the temple in Jerusalem (1 Kgs 5:1–12); however, Hiram was not too pleased with Solomon's payment for his help and called him to account (1 Kgs 9:10–14). Among the prophets, Amos (1:9–10) and Ezekiel (chapters 26–28) are the harshest in their prophecies against Tyre. Jesus and Paul visited the city.

2 Maccabees 4:18 witnesses to the fact that during Hellenistic times Tyre hosted quinquennial athletic tournaments for the entire region. Today the city is but a town known as Sur and hardly bespeaks its great history.

Sidon

Midway between Tyre and Beirut is the ancient city of Sidon, which today is known as the city of Saida, or Sayda. In many ancient documents and in the Bible, Sidon is often linked with Tyre and was overshadowed for most of its history by its neighboring city. It did, however, have a brief time of glory after the Babylonians brought Tyre under submission.

Today one can still see on a rocky small island in the Mediterranean the Crusader fortress built about A.D. 1230.

Byblos

I conclude my review of Lebanon with one of the great cities of the ancient world, the strategic port city that was called Gubla, or Gebal, among the ancients. The term *gubla* (or *gebal*) means both "hilly" and "border." The Greek merchants **corrupted the name** into *Bublos* from which comes the foundation for our current designation of the ancient city as Byblos. The Bible refers to these people as the Gebalities, or the citizens of Gebal (Ezek 27:9).

Perhaps as early as the third millennium B.C., the Egyptians were trading with the Phoenicians at Byblos for the timbers of Lebanon. Indeed, Egyptian records indicate that around 1090 B.C. Wenamon was sent on the specific mission of obtaining the finest cedars of Lebanon for the building of the sacred boat for the god Amon Re at the Temple of Thebes.

The residents of Byblos **exchanged the timber for papyrus** writing material. Here, these international traders of Gubla **invented the alphabet**. And from here **words associated with writing** came to be known as *biblos*, which was a derivative from the corrupted word *bublos* and came down to us in such words as "book," "Bible," as well as international words such as *Bibliothek*, which means "library" in German.

The site of Byblos is north of modern Beirut on a narrow plain between the Mediterranean coast and the Lebanon Mountains that provided several places for the building of harbors. The city flourished until the development of the southern harbor cities of Tyre and Sidon when it declined in importance.

Archaeologists have done one of the most extensive excavations at Byblos, beginning in 1919 under the direction of Maurice Dunand, and they have uncovered the remains of walls, residences, agora (market places), temples, and other buildings that provide significant insights into ancient life and culture. Visiting Byblos—modern Jabail—can be a fascinating experience for the students of ancient history and the biblical period.

XIII

THE CLASH OF CULTURES AND THE CLASH OF "GODS"

I F I HAVE LEARNED ANYTHING from the study of the ancient world—and having lived, studied, and taught in the lands of the Bible—it is that Christians need to understand the issues related to the clash of cultures and the relationship it bears to the clash of "gods." This concluding chapter is therefore an attempt to make clear to you, my reader, some aspects of what has taken place and what is taking place in our era today. As you read about or visit sites in the Near and Middle East related to both the past and the present, I would ask you to reflect on more than what you see or read but to consider the deeper meaning of these important sites in the overall unfolding of history.

THE GOD OF THE BIBLE AND THE "GODS" OF THE NATIONS

Ask yourself: **What was God doing** in calling "Abram" out of Mesopotamia and giving him a new name? It would no longer be the name "Abram," which meant something like "Big Daddy;" rather, it was the name "Abraham" that meant "the Father of a people"— a special people with a special purpose. We may not like to read the stories of those killings of the Canaanites, and we are clearly aware that these so-called special people—called Israel—were hardly special in their nature (like Jesus was) when it came to their actions. They obviously were sinners, and even the best of them were hardly ideal. Abraham readily used his wife to protect his own skin, and he did it not once, but twice! Jacob may have become Israel, a special prince with God, but was he really someone you would want to emulate? And David was hardly a model of morality, so how could the Bible call him a man after God's own heart? Moreover, Moses might have led the people out of their slavery in Egypt, but this murderer was not allowed to enter the Promised Land. And Elijah might have won a great victory on Mount Carmel, but it did not take him long to become a terrified fugitive. The best of them were failures. You see, as I constantly remind my students, the heroes of the Bible are not Abraham, or Jacob, or David, or Jeremiah, or Daniel—and certainly not Samson! The hero of the Bible is *God*—God who was able to use frail, fallible humans to accomplish divine purposes. And it is God who still does so today!

Did the Israelites always understand God's purposes and God's way of doing things? I doubt it! They may have killed the Canaanites but they soon adopted the

Canaanite gods! So were they any better than the Canaanites? The God of Abraham may have led them out of slavery, but they soon made a golden calf and worshiped it. They usually adopted the cultural patterns of the areas where they were and tried to join those patterns to the worship of Yahweh. They were at best syncretists like many people today. And God had God's divine hands full in trying to make them understand the great purposes of the Creator and Redeemer of the World.

So ask yourself another question: What took place on Mount Carmel? The question there was: **Who really is** *El* **("God")?** Was it *Baal* or *Yahweh?* The fire from heaven should have made that identification clear for all eternity (1 Kgs 18:17–40). Yet did it? In the clash of Yahweh with Baal, Baal lost! But unfortunately that spectacular event became merely a story for many in the history of Israel, and the people went back to syncretism.

Earlier in the time when Samuel was just becoming the prophet of Yahweh, the Israelites were losing in their battle with the Philistines, and they thought they would trump the Philistines by bringing the **ark of the covenant into battle.** They were going to **use God** for their purposes, but instead of winning the battle, they lost! Moreover, the Philistines then assumed that their culture of iron and their god Dagon was superior to the culture and God of Israel. Their culture may have been superior but their god was hardly even on a par with Yahweh because, when they placed the ark at the **foot of Dagon to humble Israel's God**, the image of their god Dagon tumbled to the ground and broke. Furthermore, the Philistines suffered from a scourge—something like boils or tumors. So the best thing, they reasoned, was to send the ark back to Israel and have **Israel's more powerful God removed** from their land (1 Sam 4:1–6:16).

You see, in those days people believed that a **god was attached to the land.** Accordingly, after Elisha told **Naaman (the Syrian general)** to wash in the Jordan and be cleansed of his leprosy, Naaman took dirt from Israel back home so that when he was back in Syria his **Israelite dirt** would indicate that he was serving Yahweh, even though he might be supporting his king in the Temple of Rimmon (2 Kgs 5:1–18). But it was not only the non-Israelites who thought that "a god" was attached to the land and therefore to the culture of the land. Even some of the Israelites espoused such a view. For example, **Jonah** was convinced that if he fled the land of Israel to Tarshish, which for him was the end of the world, then he could **get away from God.** But he found out that the God of Israel was even **God in the** *tehōm*—the Deep, or the sea, which was also identified with the place of the dead (Jon 1:3 and 2:1–10).

In terms of war, the ancients believed that the victor in a **battle** determined which **god was the strongest**; therefore, the loser in a battle was expected to acknowledge the superiority of the god who was worshiped by the victor. In many cases, refusal to **acknowledge the victor's god** assured conquered persons of death. Such a view meant that bad things or defeats should not happen to people who worship the true god, because in this way of thinking the true god must be superior to all other gods, and that superior god would will goodness for his worshipers—unless his worshipers were disobedient. Thus, one sees the significance of the incessant **probing by Job's would-be advisors** about his assumed sins or failures (Job 4ff.).

Such views continued to dominate the Mediterranean basin in the ancient world. In Egypt the pharaohs were sons of the gods and thus were themselves divine. The strength of the pharaoh and thus the strength of Egypt were attributed to **the strength of Amon, or Ra/Re.** Ramesses II was obviously blessed with the magnificence of Re and therefore was a powerful and magnificent pharaoh who had scores of wives and children to show for his blessedness. The multiplicity of wives, like the multiplicity of gods, did not trouble the ancients; their big question was which god was the most powerful at any one time. Into this context, Yahweh was introduced as the unique God, **the one and only**, which troubled the ancient mind.

An example of such a troubling of the mind occurred in Egypt when Amenophis IV changed his name to **Akhenaten** in honor of a single god "Aten," and he abandoned the historic city of Thebes where the traditional gods of the Egyptians were worshiped. Instead, he built his new capital at Tel El Amarna (Akhenaten), and he did not view himself as divine or think that human strength was an indication of integrity and piety. The reaction to such an abandonment of traditional Egyptian views was intense, and it became obvious when his son, Tutankhaten (named after Aten), changed his name to Tutankhamun (named after Amon). Then his successors sought to eliminate all remembrance of such a period in Egypt when Akehenaten and his beautiful wife Nefertiti ruled Egypt.

In the Roman period, the importance of power and strength was clearly the driving force of culture, and the **god Jupiter** was recognized as supreme in the world. But Jupiter was **not a single deity** throughout the empire. Here is the point at which many people are misled. Jupiter was the name given for any supreme deity in a culture or land, so that the Romans would have agreed to call the supreme god in Lebanon Jupiter Baal; in Israel,

Jupiter Yahweh; or in Egypt, Jupiter Ra. They all fit into the concept of a **pantheon** of the gods.

But the clash of cultures became apparent when **Pompey** marched into the Jewish temple in Jerusalem and found it empty and without a statue of Yahweh. He naturally thought that the Jews were stupid and he called them **atheists**. They had "no god!" Then Christianity came on the scene, and it confused everyone in the pagan world because not only did the Christians speak of one God but also talked about **three persons in one God**, and Jesus was the **one and only son of God** (John 1:14). Do you understand the problem the ancients had in visualizing such a phenomenon? Of course, such a problem still exists today for many people.

This single triune God, however, is the **God who gave his life for mere humans**. This God is the God that clashes with most people's view of "God." The reason is that you can never earn your acceptance with God. You can never do enough to compensate for your sinful rebellion against an utterly holy God. Acceptance by God is a gift through the death and resurrection of God's blessed Son Jesus that must be accepted by humans who believe in this redeeming act of God.

MUHAMMAD AND PERCEPTIONS OF ISLAM

Now let me fast-forward to the rise of Islam and many of the misunderstandings that have resulted in the face-off between Islam and Christianity. The issues are complex, but perhaps some brief comments can help to clarify the issue. First, let me **divide the life of Muhammad** into two segments: (a) the **Mecca Period** and (b) the **Medina Period**. In the Mecca Period, Muhammad sought to gain a hearing among his contemporaries— including some Christians—for his ideas and visions, but he was soundly rejected; in fact, his life was in peril. Accordingly, he fled to Medina, where he found refuge. Even though there he dialogued with some Christians, in reaction to his own insecurity he assumed an extremist warrior mentality that was quickly adopted by the fierce Arab tribes there. The result was that Muhammad gave them a cause for the conquest of others who did not agree with him.

It did not take long for the Arabs and their successors to **conquer** the areas controlled by the weakened **Byzantine** monarchs, and thus most of the Middle East fell before their fierce onslaught. Later the Muslims **stretched their domain** as far east as India (Pakistan) and Indonesia, as well as Afghanistan and into parts of what were some of the former Soviet Republics, especially those nations today ending with the designation "-stan." These Muslims also moved as far west as Spain and as far north as Bulgaria and into the Balkans after the fall of Constantinople. They were finally stopped in feudal Europe by Charles the Great, and little by little their dominance has yielded to the Europeans in a number of territories. But their presence is today felt throughout Europe because of immigration, and they have maintained a strong presence in the former Yugoslavia, which is now divided between Roman Catholics (Croatia), Eastern Orthodox (Serbia), and Muslims (Bosnia). After the fall of Marxism in the Balkans, the two groups of Croatia and Bosnia sought independence from the dominance of Eastern Orthodox Serbia, and the result was a major conflict in the clash of three religious cultures.

But what is crucial for readers who have not studied Muslim history to understand is that these two periods in the life of Muhammad can **still be recognized in the perspectives of Muslims.** Some are more irenic than others, and, as one should understand from my earlier brief sketches of history in the lands of the Bible, not all Muslims are the same just as not all Europeans are similar. Accordingly, just as the Germans, the French, the Spanish, and the English have had bitter fights and their periods of dominance in Europe, so the Muslims in various countries have had their periods of bitter fights and dominance in the East. Today the **Sunnis and the Shiites** are not friendly neighbors, and that fact should have been evident in the bitter wars that have occurred between Iraq and Iran in recent history. It is also true of differences between **Hamas and the Hezbollah** in the lands of Israel and Lebanon today. If one understands the so-called Six Day War, one will remember that it was in reality three two-day wars as Israel fought Egypt, then Syria, and finally Jordan. These Muslim nations acted independently, and Israel fought them independently. It is also one reason why none of the Arab nations wanted to accept the Palestinians into their nation and why the various oil-rich Arab Emirates allow other Arab visitors to come and work in their countries but do not allow them to become citizens of their countries and share in their resources. What has happened recently, however, is that **radical Islam** has been uniting various Muslims in a "jihād" perspective of eliminating the infidels for the sake of "Allah."

Now it is necessary to add a note concerning history. Because most of the history that is taught in our school systems is European and American history, we often assume incorrectly that the rest of the world was in darkness. But such is not the case. **When Europe lay in the dark period** of the Middle Ages, learning and dialoguing was taking place in other parts of the world. During this time, **Baghdad was a great center of learning** and Iman Abdu Hanifa emerged as one of the greatest scholars of this period. Others were al-Razi, al-Farabi, and al-Kindi, whose names are hardly known in the West. Indeed, the great "House of Learning" (*Baitul Hikmah*), or library, founded in the ninth century became a center for dialog between scholars—including Christians—and was a principal resource for the preservation of scores of the great classics of the earlier Greek and Roman periods after the destruction of many of the libraries in Europe.

SOME IMPORTANT QUESTIONS

The issue in the minds of most Westerners, however, has to do with the face of Islam in the present world. So, one has to **ask a number of questions.** Are all Muslims like the terrorists? The answer of course is: "No." Does the **Koran** (Qur'an) advocate the **use of violence?** The best answer is probably: "Yes." But the question could be reversed. Does the Bible advocate the use of violence? And have **Christians** believed in the **use of violence** in their purposes throughout the world? The best answer to those questions is also: "Yes—at least the Old Testament seems to support violence."

The people of Israel founded their early nation on the basis of "conquest" and violence. The modern nation-state of Israel was likewise founded on the displacement of Palestinians in a long felt view that both Christians and Muslims had earlier displaced the Jews from their lands. The violence of the Second World War and the Hitler era clearly fueled the need for a Jewish homeland safe from the discrimination of the Western world. Moreover, driven by the belief that much of the land in the Levant was a "God-given" heritage of the Jews and supported by western Europeans and many Christians particularly in the United States, the displacement of Palestinians was regarded as completely justifiable. The response to such displacement, however, has been a reactionary violence on the part of the radicals among them, which understandably birthed stepped-up security and the development of roadblocks and checkpoints with uneven treatment among people. In response to such harassment and the belief on the part of the Palestinian inhabitants that their land was taken unjustly or lost by virtue of threats from surrounding

Muslim countries, violent attacks on the Jewish inhabitants has continually increased, especially in light of continuing encroachment on additional Palestinian territories. The reaction has been the building of a new series of walls to isolate the Palestinians and to prevent their easy access to Jewish areas. The burning of forests so precious to the Jewish mindset is only another step in the downward spiral of violence in which people and nature are both sacrificed for a cause. Violence begets violence in a seemingly unending series of so-called justifiable actions on the part of injured people. Will it end soon? That question is not a simple one to answer because the gods we serve prefer violence unless it affects us.

Now ask yourself: Is **jihād** the goal of all Muslims? Well, think for a moment. Did Muslims and Christians live together in a kind of harmony in Lebanon before the influx of the Palestinians and the recent conflicts with Syria? The answer must be: "Yes." So is a **response** of violence the only way to deal with Muslims? I doubt it.

Then ask some other questions: Did Islam make great gains through the **use of the sword** in the **past** and **guns in the present?** Or, do radical Muslims use **petrochemical money** to support violence in the present era? The answer to both questions is certainly: "Yes." Has there been a clash of cultures in the past? And is there a **clash of cultures today?** The answer to both questions is: "Definitely yes." But there is also a clash between the general **Western culture and the Christian way** of life. So, do many Muslims today think of Westerners as Christian? The answer is: "Definitely yes." The **Crusades** are a vivid memory in the minds of most Muslims who identified Europe as "Christian." Remember that the fight in the Crusades was to free Jerusalem and to conquer the "infidel Muslims," and it was done under the **banner of the cross**. Many Muslims are confirmed in the view that Christians are violent people and therefore must be treated with violence. And many Christians in the West are convinced because of the radical Muslims in the world that no Muslim should be trusted. Accordingly, they would be prepared to march against the building of a mosque in their area.

But please also **remember** that much of the present view that Muslims have of Christians is also related to the **Palestinian question** and the failure of the West to take seriously the plight of the Palestinians. Of course, the **Muslims** are to a great extent **responsible** for the Palestinian problem themselves, and their goal of eliminating the Jews from Palestine. So the Palestinian problem has given the radical Muslims the tinder to ignite **their cause** of fighting against the West and their goal of eliminating the "infidels in the West" whether they are Christians, Jews, or secularists.

With these thoughts in mind, let us reflect on the clash that is present today. Muslims certainly have a historic alliance with violence and conquest, but so do Westerners! **So the question is: What kind of "God"** do many **Muslims** follow, and what kind of "God" do many **Christians** follow? This question ought to give us pause before we condemn others because maybe **our "gods"** are not too different. Moreover, maybe the critique of **Western morality** and loose living by the Muslims is justifiable. Maybe Christians have not functioned adequately as the salt within our culture to bring about the kind of transformation of morality that is necessary. Remember that where something is askew or is not treated adequately, there will almost always be an overemphasis on the other point of view. Of course, some of the Muslim identification of Western loose morality with all Christians is superficial, but maybe the Western identification of all Muslims with terrorists is also superficial.

 Now, both Islam and Christianity are concerned with winning the world. That idea is in effect a **conquest motif.** But the ultimate question is how can the world truly be won? What kind of "God" is the "God" that is honored by Christians, Muslims, and Jews? Is this God the really "unknowable one" of Islam or "the distant one" of intertestamental Judaism, or is God the one who actually made the divine self known in Jesus the Christ? Did God in Jesus the Christ actually die for mere human beings, or is God so removed as not to be personally involved in human sin and disobedience. Moreover, what kind of service of the devotees is expected from the God of the Jews and/or the God of Islam in contrast to the God and Father of Jesus the Christ? These questions are at the very heart of the clash of religions. Judaism, Islam, and Christianity all point back to Abraham, but the differences are clearly very strategic. A self-centered, narcissistic, culturally accommodating, secularized Christianity will never win the world for Jesus in the face-off with a militant Islam or any other captivating religious force. Nevertheless, to follow Jesus and his "Way" of self-giving love is not easy, yet it is ultimately the only way that does not offer a false hope to the world.

Added to this mix of the clash of religions and the old clash of cultures are the new hopes for the coming of democratic ways of life in the Near and Middle East. Many people in this countries see the freedom in the West and longingly hope and pray for it to come to them. They do not always understand what it implies—that to have freedom one must be willing to give freedom to those with whom one disagrees—but the dream has been clearly emerging there. The monarchies and dictators in this part of the world have long sought, even with violence, to quash such ideas, and they have purposely eviscerated any opposition parties that would espouse ideas of freedom and political self-determination.

Modern communication technologies, including cellular phones, Facebook, and Twitter accounts, however, have bypassed former radio and television censorship methods for controlling the dissemination of opposing views. Freedom marches and other means of expression that are used in the Wast will probably become more evident in the future. But the full results of peaceful demands for freedom are still to be seen. People's dreams can be hijacked, and visions of new ways of life are not always realized. Christians, there-fore, should earnestly pray for the people in these countries that repressive dictatorial governments and hardline Muslim takeovers of these new aspirations for freedom among the people are not sidetracked or captured by unscrupulous elements. But even more, Christians should pray for the small minority of Christians in most of these places that tthey will be sustained and emboldened to proclaim the greater freedom that is available in Jesus the Christ.

Finally, as you read your Bible and works about the religions and the history of the Middle East and, one hopes, visit the lands of the Bible in a present-day pilgrimage, please think very seriously about what kind of God actually came to these lands in his Son and provided the answer to the pains and hurts of humanity; the sins and rebellions of mankind; and to the great questions of life, death, and eternity for the entire cosmos. Is your God merely a creator who leaves your redemption up to you? Or, is your God both the Creator and the Redeemer of the world? That question requires an existential answer. Are you prepared to answer it? Are you ready to live with your answer?

ANNOTATED BIBLIOGRAPHY

I. ANCIENT AUTHORS

Ancient authors provide special insights into the lands of the Bible. Among them are Josephus, Pliny, Strabo, and Tacitus. While many translations of these writers are available, the best editions of these works are published in the Loeb Classical Library series, which are often available in university libraries. In my listing of these works, I have included the Loeb reference numbers. The following are the Loeb editions of these works:

Josephus, Flavius. *The Jewish Wars*. Translated by H. St. J. Thackery. LCL. Vols. II–IV. Cambridge, MA: Harvard University Press, 1927. [Abbreviated as *J. W.*; Loeb Classical Library, #203, 487, and 210.]

———. *Jewish Antiquities*. Translated by H. St. J. Thackery, Louis H. Feldman, Ralph Markus, and Allen Wikgren. LCL. Vols. V–XIII. Cambridge, MA: Harvard University Press, 1930–1965. [Abbreviated as *Ant.*; Loeb Classical Library, #242, 490, 281, 326, 365, 489, 410, 433, and 456.]

ALTERNATIVE SELECTIONS OF JOSEPHUS'S WORKS:

Whiston, William, trans. *The Works of Josephus*. New updated ed. Peabody: Hendrickson, 1987. [Since many people purchase a copy of Whiston's translation, I recommend it.]

Others purchase :

Williamson, G.A., trans. *The Jewish War*. Rev. ed. London: Penguin Classics, 1970.

Pliny. *Natural History*. Translated by H. Rackham, W. H. S. Jones, A. C. Andrews, and E. Eichholz. LCL. Vols. I–X. Cambridge, MA: Harvard University Press, 1938–1962. [Abbreviated as *Nat.*; Loeb Classical Library: #330, 352, 353, 370, 371, 392, 393, 418, 394, and 419.]

Strabo. *Geography*. Translated by H. L. Jones. LCL. Vols. I–VIII. Cambridge, MA: Harvard University Press, 1917–1932. [Abbreviated as *Geogr.*; Loeb Classical Library: #49, 50, 182, 196, 211, 223, 241, and 267.]

Tacitus. *Histories*. Translated by C. H. Moore, and John Jackson. LCL. Vols. II–III. Cambridge, MA: Harvard University Press, 1925–1931. [Abbreviated as *Hist.*; Loeb Classical Library: #111 and 249.]

———. *Annals*. Translated by John Jackson. LCL. Vols. III–V. Cambridge, MA: Harvard University Press, 1937. [Abbreviated as *Ann.*; Loeb Classical Library, #249, 312, and 322.]

II. FOR FURTHER READING

Many works could have been included in this list, but the following have been included for those who wish obtain further information. Readers are especially directed to the many excellent articles that appear in the issues of Biblical Archaeology Review. *This periodical provides a rich storehouse of information for those interested in subjects related to the lands of the Bible and particularly to Israel.*

Aharoni, Yohanan. *The Land of the Bible: Historical Geography*. Philadelphia: Westminster, 1980.

Avigad, Nahman. *Discovering Jerusalem*. Nashville: Thomas Nelson, 1980.

Bar-Am, Aviva. *Beyond the Walls: Churches of Jerusalem*. Jerusalem: Ahava Press, 1998.

Barakat, Akram Z. *Jordan: Special Tourism Issue*. Amman: Jordan Information Bureau, 1979.

Barrett, C. K. *The New Testament Background: Selected Documents*. New York: Harper & Row, 1961.

Batey, Richard. *Jesus and the Forgotten City*. Grand Rapids: Baker, 1995. [About the city of Zippori/Sephoris]

Borchert, Gerald L. *The Awesome Jesus: Background, Witness, and Significance*. (Macon: Mercer University Press, forthcoming.

———."Revelation." In *NLT Study Bible*. Carol Stream: Tyndale House, 2008.

Carpiceci, Alberto Carlo. *Art and History of Egypt*. Florence: Bonechi, 1994.

Connolly, Peter. *Living in the Time of Jesus of Nazareth*. New York: Oxford University Press, 1983.

Freeman-Greenville, G. S. P. *The Holy Land: A Pilgrim's Guide to Israel, Jordan and the Sinai*. New York: Continuum, 1996.

Gassir, Fouad. *Vacation in Cairo: Tourist Sites*. Cairo: Archaeological Society of Alexandria, 1988.

Gode, Hanneli. *Damascus for Tourists*. Beruit: Dar Al Anwar, 1990.

Harriz, Michel. *Baalbek: A Story in Stone*. Beruit: Harriz, n.d.

Kahen, Hasanlin Wasef. *The Samaritans: Their History, Religion, and Customs*. Nablus: Samaritan Press, n.d.

Kamil, Murad. *Coptic Egypt*. Cairo: Le Scribe Eygptien, 1968.

Mackowski, Richard M., SJ. *Jerusalem: City of Jesus*. Grand Rapids: Eerdmans, 1980.

Mazar, Amihai. "Archaeology and the Land of the Bible: 10,000–586 B.C.E." In the *Anchor Bible Reference Library*. New York: Doubleday, 1990.

Murphy-O'Conner, Jerome. *The Holy Land: An Archaeological Guide From Earliest times to 1700*. 3rd ed. Oxford: Oxford University Press, 1992.

Negev, Avraham. *Archaeological Encyclopedia of the Holy Land*. London: Weidenfeld & Nicolson, 1972.

Page, Charles R. II and Carl Volz. *The Land and the Book: An Introduction to the World of the Bible*. Nashville: Abingdon, 1993.

Pearlman, Moshe and Yaacov Yannai. *Historical Sites in Israel*. Tel Aviv: Massada Press, 1972.

Rousseau, John J. and Rami Arav. *Jesus and His World: An Archaeological and Cultural Dictionary*. Minneapolis: Fortress, 1995.

Stern, Ephraim, ed. *The New Encyclopedia of Archaeological Excavations in the Holy Land*. 4 vols. plus the supplementary 5th volume. New York: Simon & Schuster/Carta, 2006.

Vilnay, Zev. *Isarel Guide*. Jerusalem: Dal-Chen Press, 1978.

Yadin, Yigael. *Masada, Herod's Fortress and the Zealots' Last Stand*. London: Cardinal/Sphere Books, 1973.

III. MAPS AND ATLASES

The following atlases and books of maps are some works which are recommended besides the maps in most study Bibles:

Aharoni, Yohanan and Michael Avi-Yonah. *The MacMillan Bible Atlas.* New York: Macmillan, 1968. [This work with its 262 maps related to the scope of ancient empires and battles remains one of the finest one-volume resources for understanding biblical history.]

Bahat, Dan. *Carta's Historical Atlas of Jerusalem: A Brief Survey.* Jerusalem: Carta-Beit Hadar, 1973.

Baly, Dennis. *Atlas of the Bible.* New York: HarperCollins, 1997.

Beitzel, Barry. *The Moody Atlas of Bible Lands.* Chicago: Moody Press, 1985.

Cleave, Richard. *The Holy Land Satellite Atlas.* 2 vols. (Nicosia, Cyprus: Rohr Productions, 1994–1999.

Deluxe Then and Now Bible Maps. Torrance: Rose, 2010.

May, Herbert. *Oxford Bible Atlas.* New York: Oxford University Press, 1993.

Pritchard, James. *The Harper Concise Atlas of the Bible.* New York: HarperCollins, 1991.

www.ingramcontent.com/pod-product-compliance
Lightning Source LLC
Chambersburg PA
CBHW080500110426
42742CB00017B/2957